Nancy Katyal is a leang with a internationally certified executive coach and leadership development consultant with close to two decades of experience. She is also a visiting professor in top B-schools like the IIMs and MIT University. She has so far touched a million plus lives through her training, facilitation and coaching programmes across seventeen countries. Her signature programmes include:

- Executive presence/charismatic presence
- Communicating with confidence and clarity
- Decision making and critical thinking
- Leading with intention (leadership skills)
- The art of having difficult conversations
- Building self-esteem and confidence

Her clients include Fortune 500 companies, startups, luxury brands, leading corporates, celebrities, top B-schools and organisations like FICCI, CII to name a few. Nancy is president of Leadership & Mentoring Council, Maharashtra, at Women's Indian Chamber of Commerce and Industry (WICCI).

Nancy has been featured in leading national newspapers like the *Indian Express, Pune Times,* the *Times of India*, and she has been aired on radio channels too. She has many awards to her credit like the Lokmat Sakhi Sanman Award for contribution in the education sector, Limca Book of Records—National Record, Guinness World Records and fifty-one most influential women award by Brij Bhumi Foundation. She lives with her husband Vikas and daughter Ishita in Pune.

 https://www.linkedin.com/in/nancykatyal/

 @nancykatyal

PRAISE FOR THE BOOK

'I have known Nancy for over a decade now, she is a powerful personality, she has helped so many professionals and students grow in aspects and skills that are not necessarily taught in schools. From how to speak confidently to how to behave, ask for things and much more. This is a must-read book for anyone who wants to go out there in a crowded space and make their own mark. It is a quick and easy read, a guidebook of soft skills and all those required in today's time.'

— **Manish Pandey,**
content creator coach and consultant

'Nancy's book makes you realise that change is constant in everyone's life, and you can be the choreographer of change in your life. You can be the co-creator of your destiny. Make your choice and then rejoice.'

— **Dr Mickey Mehta,**
leading global holistic health guru and corporate life coach

'Through this book, Nancy provides powerful frameworks to help you build clarity in your life. An ultimate guide for those ready to do the inner work and live up to their fullest potential.'

— **Shobhit Banga,**
co-founder, Josh Talks

'I had the opportunity to interact with Ms Nancy when I was the chairperson for the IPM program at IIM R. She taught a course to our IPM students. The students absolutely loved her course and after reading the book I can understand the reasons. The book sends a positive and realistic message of self-love and self-esteem that will help people become an improved and happier version of themselves. The self-reflection exercises at the end of each chapter are well-designed to facilitate the unlearning process so necessary for self-growth and self-discovery. The writing is lucid and conveys deep insights in simple language. The author draws on her personal experiences to present deep truths in a very realistic manner. In short, the book is a helpful guide to all who believe they can improve themselves.'

— **Dr Sanket Sunand Dash,
assistant professor, IIM Rohtak and chairperson,
Placement Committee (2022–23)**

'This book is the best friend you need to create an inner shift and lead the life you desire. What we're taught in schools and colleges clearly aren't taking us anywhere, we need a blueprint and guide to help us solve complex challenges of life. The book is a must-read for students, corporate professionals or anyone who is serious about reinventing themselves and who want to create an inner shift. This is a must-read for everyone who wants to increase their self-awareness and unleash their true potential. The book is a blueprint to leading a fulfilling life as it helps you become the best version of yourself.'

— **Dr Ritesh Malik,
founder, Innov8 and trustee, Plaksha University**

'Is loving oneself an act of selfishness? Do we value ourselves enough? Infused with experiential wisdom, this book is an invitation to create respect and love for oneself. In this book, Nancy has given a new thinking model for individuals. A must-read for anyone who wants to work on their self-confidence and transform their lives.'

— **Shailesh Sharma,**
director-Manufacturing, SKF India and South East Asia

'A must-read influential guide written by Nancy Katyal with great simplicity that instantly builds a positive connection with your own self and helps you get out of your own way through practical proven frameworks.'

— **Sawaisingh Rajpurohit,**
director-Payments Technology, Barclays

'Anyone who is curious about life, change and wants to be MAD (make a difference), this is your go-to book! It is a reminder to you about you and why it is worth every bit just reading. There's something for everyone across generations.'

— **Rajita Singh,**
head HR, Broadridge

'If you are serious about your personal growth, then you can't miss reading this book.'

— **Abhishek Suryawanshi,**
founder-director, Wikipedia SWASTHA

'Nancy Katyal addresses some key issues that we all face today and most importantly, deep dives into how we can understand ourselves better and emerge victorious. Read this book to learn from one of the best!'

— **Parzaan Dastur,**
filmmaker and actor

'You don't only read this book, this book talks to you! This book introduces you to a "new you", a more mindful version of yourself. Through this book, Nancy has made some amazing life lessons extremely easy to understand and relatable that they'll stay with you for a very long time.'

— **Shakeel Ahmad,**
an edupreneur and co-founder of Mind Mingle,
and Spark Astronomy

'This book opens up in front of you like a mirror. It makes you realise, "Hey, it happened to me also and that's exactly how I felt." It is these relatable snippets of life along with practical frameworks which Nancy has brought out so beautifully in the book that makes this book stand out. A must-read if you want to know yourself better and bring in a change.'

— **Uddalak Chatterjee,**
senior vice president and head-branch operations and
operations training, Bajaj Allianz Life Insurance Co. Ltd

'A book that anyone can easily relate to—be it for your personal or professional life. If you are someone who is looking to strive for your personal growth, then this book is a handy guide with practical steps and strategies. A game changer!'

— **Varun Patil,**
senior HR Leader

'This book inspires us to live an exponential life and to unleash our extraordinary self. Go get your copy.

— **Shweta A. Chaudhary,**
Mrs India Earth and influencer

'If you aspire to live an exponential life, then this book is your go-to guide for life.'

Deepika Singh,
popular actress

'Through the book, Nancy speaks to the person inside us; what we face every day, what we need to do about it and why the answer lies with no one but us. She uses hard-hitting real-life scenarios and stories to share lessons. It's an extremely well-researched and insightful book and reading it makes you feel like having a personal coach hand-holding you to become a person you always wanted to be. A must-have for professionals who want to cut through the noise and look for practical frameworks and a very actionable and achievable plan to have fulfilment in their life.'

— **Ajit Sharma,**
TEDx ambassador and former TED Talks India coach

'There is countless literature available online and offline talking about how to lead self. I won't be able to find a single person who doesn't want to be a good leader. But while we whole-heartedly dive deep down into reading about self-leadership skills, we forget about a very important aspect of leading self-CHANGE. Change and willingness to adapt to the external as well as the internal environment is vital to be a good leader and Nancy in her book sets the premise of this exceptionally well-structured read on the importance of change. While she throws light on her personal experiences to cement her thoughts, she not only shares valuable theories, but also picks up the conversation from this very important aspect. If you are ready to change, congratulations, you have started your journey to become an exceptional leader.'

— **Kshitij Garg,**
managing director, Estero

'Nancy has simply yet elegantly shown the importance of self-love. By citing incidents from her rich experience and sharing simple analogies, tools and strategies, she has attempted to stress with readers how to seek inner inspiration instead of seeking outside approval, constantly challenge oneself and give credit for smaller wins. The readers will be compelled to reflect and learn to Love Thyself along with learning to enjoy the journey and efforts taken towards the ultimate goal.'

— **Shilpa Kotwal,**
digital delivery lead, Amdocs

'A must-read if you need a new dimension of perception to rediscover yourself. This book also inspires you to fall in love with yourself and is a game changer if you want to grow and transform.'

— **Manoneet Mathur Sindhu,**
fashion stylist and socialite

'Nancy provides an unpretentious tool for us to navigate our inner world. Her guidance is non-judgemental in a way that she helps readers achieve a level of self-acceptance of the struggle through a lot of self-disclosure of her own metamorphosis—a way of role modelling technique. This requires another level of courage and confidence. That is what she intends for the readers.'

— **Dr Lakshmi Kumar,**
founder director, The Orchid School
and inter-cultural coach, Sweden-India Project

'Through her book, Nancy prescribes a workbook approach to self-development and living your best self. Her writing style is simple and effective. She shares frameworks and tools that can help you reach your true potential.'

— **Minaxi Indra,**
president, upGrad for Business

'As a reader, I was drawn into this very practical, insightful, gem of a book. Nancy's writing is lucid, perceptive, interspersed with reflective anecdotes and personal experiences. As a storyteller she elevates you with the right dose of motivation, holding space for the reader, inviting them to become better versions of themselves with curiosity, empathy and connection. It's a book to be read and reread and dog-eared, a book where you can come home to yourself. A delightful read!'

— **Mrunal Pawar,**
director, Sakal Media Group

COMMIT TO
YOURSELF
BREAK FREE

NANCY KATYAL

Om Books International

Reprinted in 2023 by

Om Books International

Corporate & Editorial Office
A-12, Sector 64, Noida 201 301
Uttar Pradesh, India
Phone: +91 120 477 4100
Email: editorial@ombooks.com
Website: www.ombooksinternational.com

Sales Office
107, Ansari Road, Darya Ganj,
New Delhi 110 002, India
Phone: +91 11 4000 9000
Email: sales@ombooks.com
Website: www.ombooks.com

ISBN: 978-93-95701-46-4

Printed in India

10 9 8 7 6 5 4 3 2

To

All those who continue to believe in hope
and look at their failures with as much pride
as their successes.

——

All the people who believed in me and also to those
who didn't; all those moments of self-doubt, self-
blame and shame; the moments of triumph over
self-limiting thoughts to letting go of connections,
thoughts and things that did not serve me for my
highest good—it was in those moments that I took
the first step to create that inner shift.

Contents

Chapter 2: From 'Hole' to Being Whole 19
The Journey Explained

Chapter 3: Untie the Knots of Your Mind 41
Break Free

Chapter 6: How to Create an Inner Shift

The Journey Explained

Chapter 7: To a More Courageous And an Authentic You

Right Here, Right NOW

DEAR READER...

There is a reason you have picked this book. You know that feeling when you wanted to make a change in yourself but somehow kept postponing it? You were committed to helping others, being there for them at all times, but somehow fell short of giving the same commitment to yourself. Sounds familiar? Well, you have neglected your needs long enough, high time you reclaim yourself back.

We all have certain areas in our life that are not functioning to its optimum capacity. This book shares practical strategies, proven frameworks and tools that can help you to move from *where you are to where you want to be* and live your life by freeing yourself from old patterns of behaviour and find the courage to let go of things that do not serve you any more.

Many of us fail to realise that sometimes we are our biggest hurdle and distraction in realising our full potential. Hence, it is no coincidence that the word 'improvement' begins with the alphabet 'I'.

This book is a labour of my love after seven years of intense research and interviewing people from different walks of life. I have in this book shared with you what helped people when they were unhappy with themselves to ultimately following practical and easy-to-implement strategies to fall in love with themselves, fall in love with their work and more importantly, fall in love with life.

Hey, I am sure this thought just crossed your mind: *I know, I know I need to change, I will do that at some point in my life…*

Well, may I just interrupt your mind chatter for a second? Just to remind you, you have only one life. Also, in order for things to change outside of you, they must first change within you.

Remember the aircraft safety briefing?

'If you are travelling with children, make sure that *your own mask* is on first before helping your children.' Similarly, when you add value to yourself, you become more valuable and then you are in a better position to add more value to others. When you take ownership and responsibility and say to yourself, '**I** am accountable for the change in my life', magic happens.

If this speaks to you, welcome onboard on the journey of breaking free from your self-imposed chains and unlocking your true potential by creating an *inner shift*. I am honoured to be your co-pilot on this journey.

INTRODUCTION

'Life is available only in the present moment.'

—Thich Nhat Hanh

WAKE UP!

And smell the coffee. Before it is *too* late.

Sometimes, a particular incident or even just a couple of words shake you to the core. It is in that moment when these words start to echo in your mind, as if someone is, standing close to you, grabbing your shoulders, shaking you and shouting at the top of their lungs, 'WAKE UP!'

There comes a point in time when your inner voice tells you, 'Enough is enough' and it is in that moment your heartbeat races and you feel a shiver down your spine, making you realise that something has shifted within you. As your heartbeat returns to normal, you look at life and the people around you in a slightly different way now. You want more from life. High time! In just one instance, so many things change for you at so many levels. It is like a whole different spin on the eureka moment. Have you ever had such a moment? I did.

My eureka moment

I had my first eureka moment in 2005 when our daughter Ishita was born. Every time I saw her calm face and hazel green eyes, I felt elated to know that a life came through me.

My close family members could not contain their happiness either. I cannot say the same about the rest of my family members though. Because slowly, many of my relatives started whispering in hush tones, saying, 'Oh...but the baby is a girl...'

The day I got wind of the whisper campaign I was deeply hurt and disappointed.

How could people be displeased with the gender of a newborn? And *continue* to offer their fake congratulations! How could people say that my girl would not amount to anything? Especially in this modern age when girls are heading multinational corporations, leading nations and charting spaceships!

I heard them. I heard them well. I heard them loud.

But said nothing. And by doing so, I failed to take charge of the moment, or of my life. Instead, I acted as if nothing had happened and repeatedly told myself these things do not impact me, and continued living my life. But still somehow deep down I felt someone had put a heavy weight on my heart. It was my baby they were talking about. I *had* to act.

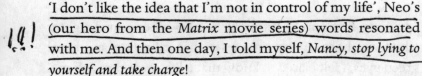

'I don't like the idea that I'm not in control of my life', Neo's (our hero from the *Matrix* movie series) words resonated with me. And then one day, I told myself, *Nancy, stop lying to yourself and take charge*!

You know that feeling when you are exhausted of pretending to be a 'nice person'? Deep down, I knew that my way of handling things was not helping me lead the life that I wanted. All I needed was that 'eureka moment'. And I finally got mine.

I am sure you too have experienced situations when you felt frustrated and underconfident, when you wanted to speak your heart out or just wanted to seek help but somehow were unable to gather the courage to speak your truth. Remember that raise you asked for and did not get? Or the promotion? Or the date? And even when you made an attempt, it did not help; in fact, it backfired. Practically everything that could have gone wrong, went wrong. In those moments, you begin to think that there is something definitely wrong with *you*. And you begin to wonder why you are being misunderstood, or why people take you for a ride always. As you go down the rabbit hole, you start believing that *you* are part of the problem. But the problem continues when you go down in this negative spiral of overthinking about the problem alone, instead of facing the problem eye-to-eye and thinking about the solution or seeking support from others or a professional.

One size does not fit all

I am sure you have attended dozens of self-improvement workshops or read loads of self-help books, only to be left with an overflowing bookshelf and a confused state of mind. And there is only one burning question that still remains in your mind: *Why are things not changing around you?* And you keep asking yourself: *Why do I say yes when I want to say no?*

Why am I not taking action that is useful for my own life?! *Oh God, why?* Advice from friends, family members or motivational speakers may be the most well-meaning of all, but you need to understand that something that has worked for someone else, will necessarily work for you.

One size does not fit all, my friend!

It is your life. Live it your way.

'If nothing changes, nothing changes'

Growth does not happen by just having good intentions. For instance, you want to drive from Pune to Mumbai. However, just having the desire to drive will not take you to Mumbai. You need to get off your ass first, find the car keys (wherever the hell they are), get into your car, start the engine, start driving till you reach your destination with short halts in-between—for chai and sandwich of course. Now, that is called action. I know this sounds so basic, but that is just how simple it is.

Be the change-maker in your life.

This journey of freeing yourself from old habits and patterns of behaviour cannot be taken in a bullet-train mode, it has to be in a slow mode. *The journey is more important than the destination.*

Hey, look, this book will be of no use to you if you do not *commit* to implementing the strategies and tools shared in it because *'if nothing changes, nothing changes'* to quote the best-selling author Courtney C. Stevens.

I know, I know. Commitment is the BIG 'C' word that most of you want to avoid. However, we will inevitably repeat old patterns unless we awaken and commit to taking the first step towards change.

Let me make this easier for you. Take one baby step at a time. At the end of each chapter, you will get the opportunity to jot down your thoughts, please take a moment to write your responses in the self-enquiry zone. It takes time to create that much needed inner shift because knowing something intellectually is one thing and experiencing it personally and taking an action on that awareness is altogether a different thing.

Read the book to deeply connect with yourself. It will definitely inspire you to connect with the loving, warm, wiser, awesome and joyful side of you.

The *promise* that you need to make to yourself

I know that 'promise' is often a misused word, but if you diligently and consistently implement the frameworks discussed in the book and write down your thoughts, you will automatically be working towards your progress, one day at a time. Research has proven that whenever we write something down, we tell our brain that it is important and most importantly we begin to see in front of us what is working and what is not. According to a 2014 study by researchers from Princeton and University of California, Los Angeles (UCLA), using your phone or laptop to take notes will not help to absorb the material well, rather writing down your own notes, helps you to process things better and improve your memory.[1]

I can assure you, if not 'promise', that each sincere step you take towards bettering yourself will not only bring you closer to having a beautiful and healthy relationship with yourself, but also with people around you.

Trust the process. Trust is the gift you give to others, only after you have given it to yourself.

1. Pam A. Mueller and Daniel M. Oppenheimer, sagepub.com, 2014, https://linguistics.ucla.edu/people/hayes/Teaching/papers/MuellerAndOppenheimer2014OnTakingNotesByHand.pdf, accessed on 28 July 2022.

Please use the space below to jot down three commitments you are meaning to make for your personal growth.

I commit to myself that...

....

....

....

....

....

....

....

....

....

....

1

TAKE A LEAP OF FAITH

Embrace Change

'I crossed the street to walk in the sunshine.'

—Elizabeth Gilbert

Have you ever wondered why things do not work out the way you want?

Why do you struggle to form daily habits?

Why do some people seem to be 'lucky', and not you? !!!

Why are some people happier, more productive, more fulfilled than you?

Why do some people seem to be at ease with themselves?

Have you wondered why you keep asking yourself these questions?

The answer is simple: you are looking for quick fixes to handle your problems because deep down you, like many others, believe that there must be a quick-fix solution to get what you want. I do not blame you. You are hardwired to do things that are comfortable for you like most of us. Just the thought of bringing in a change in your life can feel burdensome because it is so much easier to stay in your comfort zone. But then as the famous author and screenwriter, Neale Donald Walsch, once said, 'Life begins at the end of your comfort zone.'

And I am sure you too must have had those moments when you said, 'From tomorrow I will start working on the NEW version of me. I will wake up early, only eat healthy food, exercise regularly and make more time for my family.' But guess what? When that alarm clock rings in the morning, you conveniently press snooze, and continue dozing.

I do not blame you.

You live in a culture where you (like the rest of us) are constantly being bombarded with messages claiming that 'this revolutionary product' will help you get that waistline in ten days, or you can become successful in seven steps, or heal yourself with 'this online course'. But all this is just a facade. Because change takes time. Especially when it is behavioural. As someone perfectly describes this dilemma— 'Even hurry takes time'. Breakthrough moments are usually the result of actions taken over time.

I was once conducting a workshop with senior leaders of an IT company, wherein I gave them an exercise to write down an aspect of their life that they were finding hard to change, and also write down a solution that could be the catalyst for that change.

A young gentleman from the audience stood up and said, 'Change is not possible.'

I could see the unrest in his body and voice.

I asked him, 'Did you ever imagine that your parents will use netbanking even though they told you only a few years ago that it is extremely unsafe and they only believe in cash transactions?'

He paused and replied, 'Oh yes! They now order most of their stuff from Amazon and several other online platforms using their card.'

He then nodded and a smile broke on his face. He said, 'Thank you, got that.'

You do not have to take gigantic steps to usher in change in your life—do not underestimate the <u>ability of tiny wins every</u> day. Sometimes the biggest obstacle that comes in your way is YOU. The single biggest lie you tell yourself is 'I cannot change NOW, or I am too OLD to do this.'

Giving up is NOT the solution

A .... B C

Confused?

Do not be.

Let us deconstruct this. Imagine C is the final destination you want to reach. Is it possible for you to jump from A to C without going through B? Unless you are a long jumper like Mike Powell or Murali Sreeshankar, of course not! A mindful and an aware person does not look at Point C as their final destination. Instead, they tell themselves, *Today I'm at Point A, I have the potential to be at Point B in a certain amount of time and with continued effort, I will reach Point C.*

Relax!

You will get there—that is, to being a mindful and an aware person.

What you essentially need to do is to take the staircase. As much as you would love to use the elevator, the stairs also take you from one floor to another floor gradually and does not just go zoooooom to reach the third floor. It is just a matter of effort. Growth requires practising habits every day consistently. You just cannot lose weight by eating junk food for five days at a stretch and nutritious food for the remaining two days of the week, right?

What if eating nutritious food for a week still did not give you the results you were hoping for? Would you give up? Well, you see that is the problem—you, like many, will give up trying something if it does not work out once or twice. And this process of trying and failing can be emotionally draining. Hence, many people do not even try to go through the journey. But *you* will not be one of them.

Why?

Because you are reading this book.

I once received an incredible piece of advice from a hugely successful person, who seemed to echo what many successful people have told me several times in the past—'The moment you feel like giving up is the moment you need to try once more. But you must be wondering, *What about those successful people who simply got lucky and those so-called celebrities who became famous overnight?*

Valid question. Let me explain.

Luck re-defined

I remember back in 2016 Ishita, all of eleven years, had just finished delivering her talk at the TED Global Conference in Vancouver, and we decided to sit in the lobby area to celebrate her incredible feat. She was then the youngest Indian TED speaker. A lady walked up to me, and said, 'Your daughter is lucky she got to do this.'

That is when a stranger standing next to me promptly said, 'Isn't it strange that without knowing the background, we are quick to unfairly consider some people as "lucky". How do I view "luck"? For me luck is learning under correct knowledge.'

Interesting outlook. Don't you think?

Every single step you take every day will take you closer to your goal. This reminds me of what the founder and executive chairman of Amazon Jeff Bezos once famously said, 'All overnight success takes about ten years.'

Okay, maybe ten years is a stretch. I will get you there quicker.

Destiny does not change in one day, but it does change some day! And the day it changes is often due to the consistent efforts taken over a period of time.

There is no such thing as an overnight success. It is so easy to shift the focus on luck, rather than acknowledging the effort and hard work put behind the success. Sometimes a two-hour-long movie could take two years to put together. Have you ever thought about that? All you do is munch your popcorn, sip your favourite drink, watch the movie and say, 'Okay well, that was that. Let's go.'

It is okay. That is not a crime, but do inculcate the habit of appreciating the efforts put behind others' achievements and strive to put in some hard work to improve your 'luck'.

Stop living the BIG, FAT LIE

Sometimes you may wonder why you did not write that email or followed a particular diet, or made that phone call. Was it ego? Did not want to live through the pain again? Or was it sheer laziness? Remember, everything you do will only bring you closer to what you truly desire and deserve, and this in turn will bring about a shift in the way you see the world and yourself.

Like many others, you too are comfortable living your life no matter how dissatisfied you are with it. All it takes is that first step to commit to taking charge of your life, and ushering in change for good. Do not underestimate your own potential. You may think that the process is a painful one but write that email, make that phone call, follow the healthy diet and notice the difference. Every step you take will not only bring you closer to reaping fruitful results in your life, but also bring about a shift in the way you view the world and yourself. And a new perspective of looking at issues has the possibility of turning your life around.

'Great things are done by a series of small things brought together', so said the genius artist Vincent Van Gogh.

You need a plan

Just like you cannot skip chapters when you are reading a book, you cannot skip the important chapters in your life, that is *not* how life works. You have to read every line, every paragraph, live through every plot twist and meet every character in your life. You may not enjoy all of it, but you have to keep going. Trust me, it is worth it.

The notion that you can change your life in a day is a BIG, FAT LIE. As the famous saying goes: Rome was not built in a day. The day you plant the seed is not the day you eat the fruit...

There must be so many things that you want to do to break the old, unhealthy pattern but where do you begin? Wondering how to take the first step?

How many times have you heard 'Just believe in yourself'? Has it worked? Sometimes, perhaps. Have all those self-help books, well-meaning podcasts worked? Clearly not. Otherwise you would not be holding this book. Right? But stop for a moment and reflect.

Why are you *still* seeking solutions?

Several studies show that external solutions are temporary. You try a particular diet for a few days, try exercising for a month to bring in the much required and eagerly anticipated change. And then BOOOOM! Something happens and you are back to square one. You sit and ponder *yet again* why you did not get what you wanted. The answer is simple: You need a plan, my friend. A framework or a model that can give you a step-by-step approach to help you start your engine. Ignite the fire in your belly.

Do not worry, I have got you covered.

What is your relationship status with *yourself*?

As I was researching for this book, I spoke to many successful people, and I started noticing a startling pattern emerging—truly successful people are able to lead their lives without fear, and are able to cut the outside noise and lead their lives with joy and peace. As you dive deeper into the book, you will understand the reason behind this. But let me just build some suspense for now. Suspense is a real beast, I know!

First step?

Sit straight!

Now think about the most important relationship in your life. No, this is not about your bae. This is about YOU. *The relationship that you have with yourself.* Yes, you heard (rather read) that right. You are in a relationship with yourself first.

On the note of having a great relationship with yourself, I recall a workshop I facilitated way back in 2012 in Mumbai. I asked the participants to mention the names of people who contributed to their journey so far.
Pause. Think.

How you would have answered this question?

Well, if you are like most people who were present there, you would name your mum or dad or teacher/mentor or friend, or worst critic, etc. But no one ever really says, 'I, Me'. Of course, having humility is one thing. But it is a completely different thing to not say that *you* too are responsible for where you have reached today and should be proud of all the choices you made along the way. *No, I am not talking about all those wrong decisions you made when you got drunk.* But then you live and learn.

You must have been often given the advice to become self-aware. Unfortunately, simply being self-aware is not an effective solution. Self-awareness alone does not help, you need to take an action. You realise what you are doing. You vow to change it and never repeat it. (You hold the best of intentions.) But then, to your dismay, you find yourself engaging in the same destructive behaviour over and over again.

But no, you are not the problem. So do not beat yourself down.

The problem is the method that you have adopted. Clearly, that has not worked for you till date. The results are the proof; you want your life to be better.

I am sure, you too like the rest of us have one aspect in your life that is not functioning at an optimal level. Perhaps, your bae is driving you mad, or you cannot stand to be in your skin any more. (Remember, you have a relationship with yourself *too!*). Or maybe you feel underappreciated at work. Or your bank balance has gone kaput.

Even when everything seems right, you may just have a sense of emptiness and yearn for a deeper, more fulfilling experience. This lack of fulfilment is because you, like a lot of us, have just not found the tools that you need to create the life you know you deserve. But there is good news. There is always good news. And the good news is that there are practical and easy-to-apply tools that can facilitate true transformation in any aspect of your life.

Phew! Finally, you see the light at the end of the rather long tunnel. Keep walking (or reading).

Learning to love yourself starts with identifying your own set of beliefs about yourself and removing the ones that do not serve you. First learn to trust yourself enough to say, 'I MATTER'. It is only when you do not have a solid relationship with yourself, you will lean on others for approval.

'It's not your job to like me…it's mine!' Byron Katie

She got that right.

Pause. Think.

Do you have a good relationship with yourself? What is the relationship status: detached, clueless, in love or out of love? Let us leave it at complicated. Shall we?

But not for long. It certainly will not be by the time you are through with this book.

Towards your cherished goal: one step at a time

In reality, all that you need is within you, but it just gets lost in the mess since you do not have a clear picture. Let me explain this. I call it The Staircase Approach because 'there is no elevator to success, you have to take the stairs.' (Zig Ziglar)

Staircase Approach

Visualise this: You are living in a four-storied apartment building and your flat is on the third floor. As you take your first step from the ground floor (you are not taking the lift because you are taking things slow now), none of the floors above are visible to you. As you take more steps, you begin to get a glance of the first floor. And once you take a few more steps, the entire first floor is entirely visible to you. (Now, I know you are thinking, *Duh, Nancy*, but just stay with me. Please.) At this point, you are aware that you still have one more floor to cross till you reach your destination. But with every set of steps, no matter how mundane they might be, you get rewarded slowly and steadily. Because all your consistent efforts lead you to your final destination.

So here is the deal. Make a pact with yourself:

- I will move beyond my obstacles,
- I will strive to achieve my goals,
- I will no longer be comfortable with things that are not serving me well and
- I will unlock my greatness.

One step at a time.

Change can be easy and fun, provided you commit to doing the best you can. The secret lies in the choices that you make every single day, right from the moment you wake up till the moment you hit the bed.

You have to do your own push-ups, as no one else can do it for you. Not everything can be outsourced even in this day and age. The inner shift is not as hard as you think. Take the leap of faith. Because 'first, you leap, and then you grow wings', as the legendary social activist William Sloane Coffin once said.

So, fill your cup of self-love to the brim and take one sip at a time because 'loving yourself isn't vanity. It's sanity.' (Andre Gide)

Identify your obstacles and what is that first step that you can take towards overcoming them?

....

....

....

....

....

....

....

....

....

....

2

FROM 'HOLE' TO BEING WHOLE

The Journey Explained

'Wholeness does not mean perfection: it means embracing brokenness as an integral part of life.'

—Parker J. Palmer

November 2016, an incident happened that brought a major shift in how I looked at myself and others around me. I entered a training room as an attendee and picked a close spot to the front. The speaker began the session by waving a 2,000-rupee currency note at us, asking everybody, 'What is the value of this note?'

Everyone smiled, shrugged their shoulders and said in unison, '2000 rupees.'

The trainer chuckled and said, 'It's obvious that the value is Rs 2,000, isn't it?'

He then proceeded to crumple up the note and asked us what would be its value now? We all agreed that the value was still the same. He then threw the note on the ground and asked us with fervour, 'Is the value still the same?'

Everyone in the room responded with a resounding, 'YES'!

What he said next has stayed with me for all these years.

He said, 'I held up this note in its perfect condition and yet the value remained the same even when it looked crushed, wrinkled and flawed. So why is it that most of us tend to undermine our value? Circumstances may jolt you, mould you but your value doesn't decrease based on someone's inability to see your worth. So why is it that most of us tend to undermine our value? You are priceless.'

Voila! There was complete silence in the room. I felt as if the trainer was looking right into my eyes and reminding me of how I had treated myself badly based on what others thought of me. It also dawned on me how I had unfairly compared my life with others without realising that everyone has a different life journey.

As the popular saying goes, 'Everybody is a genius. But if you judge a fish by its ability to climb a tree, it will live its whole life believing that it is stupid.'

As I looked around the room, I saw some people smiling with gratitude, some were teary-eyed while others looked surprised, pursing their lips and wondering why they had not realised this before. But in the end, each person sitting in that room could feel a shift within.

I am sure that at some point of time in your life, you too would have thought less about yourself based on someone else's opinion of you. If someone does not like what you said, you might chide yourself and feel bad. But if someone rejects you, does that mean you should reject yourself? The simple and obvious answer is NO. But not many know this. Why is it so difficult for you to accept yourself fully? It is because of your conditioning.

Why should someone's opinion of you have to become your reality?

Here is an exercise for you to do:

Write down your instant response to the given scenarios:

A: Your friend walks up to you and says, 'I don't like your bag.'

_____

_____

_____

_____

B: Your friend walks up to you and says, 'I love you.'

_____

_____

_____

_____

_____

Try to see what contrast exists between the two responses. Which statement are you more likely to believe? Which one will you feel the most?

It is natural to first doubt love shown by others and instantly accept criticism without blinking an eyelid. Have you ever stopped to think about why you do that?

Start a life-long romance with yourself: break-up is not an option

Quite a few of us tend to prioritise others' feelings and welfare over our own needs, thinking that self-care is a selfish act. Women, especially Indian mothers, suffer from this martyr complex. We struggle to keep our needs before others because it is deeply rooted in our upbringing. We have taken for granted the sacrifices of those who raised us and internalised them. *Loving yourself is not an act of selfishness*. One of my favourite quotes by Caroline Caldwel echoes this thought—'In a society that profits from your self-doubt, liking yourself is a rebellious act.'

And now you may ask yourself: *How do I avoid being self-obsessed? How do I maintain a balance between taking care of myself and others?*

It is pretty simple. Maintain a love account just like you manage your bank account.

Open a love account

Imagine that you have opened your love account in the Love Bank. If you keep withdrawing love from your account and sharing it with others very soon you will have zero balance in your love account, and you will have nothing left for yourself or others. Whereas, if your account is filled with love, you will be in a better position to offer it to others too. As the old saying goes, you cannot pour from an empty cup.

Or to use the modern lingo, 'Self-care is the greatest middle finger of all time.'

But do remember, loving yourself does not mean disregarding others; on the contrary, when you accept and love yourself fully, you are in a better position to accept and love others fully. The more you love yourself, the more likely you are to treat others with respect, kindness and love.

When I bring out the best in me, I am able to bring out the best in you.

IF-only syndrome: the new malaise

The reality is that the majority of us do not really love ourselves fully and it is not that we do it knowingly or do not want to love ourselves. One of the biggest problems that comes in our way is the 'IF-only syndrome'.

> IF only I could afford that exotic vacation…
>
> IF only I lose ten kilos…
>
> IF only I could get a bigger car…
>
> IF only I am promoted to a better position…

only then am I praiseworthy or loveable or whole.

You are whole and complete as you are, external validation will not enhance your self-esteem rather, the time and effort you make for your self-care and personal growth is what will truly make a difference.

'ME Time' beyond binging

There is a lot of chatter on social media on self-care or 'ME Time'. Self-care is often linked with salon visits or pampering yourself by going on shopping sprees, or binge-watching a show, or binging. Some people indulge in certain activities in the name of self-care and at times, it is at the cost of going over and above their realistic budget.

They buy into this false idea that because they have the means to afford a particular thing, they will begin to feel good about themselves after acquiring it. We also tend to link our self-care with our self-esteem. There is nothing wrong in indulging yourself once in a while to fulfil your desires, but when you attach these desires to your self-worth, you harm yourself.

Self-care is what is needed for your overall well-being. Self-care improves both your physical and mental health. The four powerful ways to practice self-care:

Moving around

Any form of movement, be it exercising, walking, dancing, etc., is good for your mind and body. Just ten minutes of any kind of movement significantly improves your focus and reduces burnouts.

Spending time in nature

Some of us lead a sedentary lifestyle and spend most of our time indoors. Spending time amidst nature and stepping out of our cocoon or comfort zone improves your mental health, boosts your creativity and reduces stress.[1]

---

1. BMC Public Health, 'Exploring the beliefs and perceptions of spending time in nature among U.S. youth', 23 August 2021, https://bmcpublichealth. biomedcentral.com/articles/10.1186/s12889-021-11622-x, accessed on 30 August 2022.

Indulging in creative activities

Think of the activities you enjoyed doing as a kid. Maybe you liked painting or listening to music or writing. Awakening the inner child in you is a great form of self-care.

Being compassionate to yourself

Spending time with yourself in silence and observing your thoughts without any judgment allows us to be kind to ourselves. Giving yourself a compassionate virtual hug when you feel stressed and also seeking out help when you feel lost or are in pain is the best form of self-care.

Activities related to self-care are personal to each one of us. Choose those activities that help you to restore and rejuvenate your physical and mental well-being.

To be or not be *complete?*

Advertising companies are aware of the fact that it is a human tendency to look at oneself as 'hole' (incomplete) whereas people aspire to see themselves as 'whole' (complete). Therefore, advertisements are directed towards selling you a promise: a promise that a cream will make you look flawless, a promise that buying a product will make you happier and complete you. As Will Rogers once famously said, 'Advertising is the art of convincing people to spend money they don't have for something they don't need.'

Posts by your 'social circle' on social media often make you feel that something is missing in you or in your life. Think about how often you have based your worth in the hands of others. I am sure there are times when you suffer from FOMO (fear of missing out) like many others. What steps have you taken to overcome that? Have you ever looked at it from a different perspective instead of FOMO, how about POMO—pleasure of missing out. You do not have to participate in every circus that goes around to fit in and feel whole.

The truth is that you are 'whole' already. Wholeness comes with accepting and embracing your imperfections as well as accepting your strengths.

You do not necessarily need a product or service to make yourself feel complete. Making informed choices while buying something because you need to is different from buying something because you think you lack something and you just need to fill the void.

One question that I find extremely powerful to help you understand the relationship you share with yourself is: How do you view yourself?

Do you have a tendency to focus only on the hole (your flaws) in yourself, or do you acknowledge and appreciate who you are completely as a whole along with your flaws?

Do you want to be incomplete or complete? It is really not Sophie's choice actually. It is a pretty simple choice. Choose to be whole.

And seeking wholeness does not mean seeking perfection. Being 'whole' means accepting who you are and being aware that you have the potential to become the best version of yourself without putting yourself down.

I do understand that when you wake up in the morning and look at yourself in the mirror there are parts of you that you may not like and you see them as your imperfections, but loving yourself means accepting your imperfections as well. Your hair might be a mess or your skin might be breaking out, but you are still as meaningful and important.

It is amusing to notice how these delicate surfaces of glass brought about such a huge change in our lives especially in our perception of ourselves. But it is even more amusing to see how we have managed to turn such a wonderful invention into a mass insecurity.

You don't have to try so hard
You don't have to give it all away
You just have to get up, get up, get up, get up
You don't have to change a single thing...
You don't have to try, try, try, try
You don't have to try, try, try, try
You don't have to try
You don't have to try

Take your make up off
Let your hair down
Take a breath
Look into the mirror, at yourself
Don't you like you?
Cause I like you

These lyrics from Colbie Caillat's song (one of my favourites) *'Try'* pretty much sums up what I am trying to convey here.

To add to the above, wholeness is not just about accepting your physical flaws, it is also about forgiving yourself for past actions that you are particularly not proud of because that was the best awareness you had at that time. *Wholeness encompasses your darkness and your light.*

'Wholeness is not achieved by cutting off a portion
of one's being, but by integration of the contraries.'

—Carl Gustav Jung

Wise words from the world-renowned psychiatrist and psychoanalyst.

There are two ways to look at anything, either you change what you do not like, or accept it if you cannot change it. The moment you begin to accept the parts that you were rejecting earlier, you will begin to get more confident and comfortable with your body and yourself. You will begin to build a more harmonious relationship with yourself and will be motivated to bring changes that are in your control. For instance, if you do not like that you are unfit, you will begin to exercise. If you do not like the way you speak to others, you will be more mindful to gather your thoughts before speaking the next time.

You are confined only by the walls you *choose to* build around yourself. Never forget, everything in life is temporary, whatever you are struggling with today, will be gone tomorrow. So, you do not have to become a hostage to your past.

There is a saying attributed to the Buddha, 'Nothing can harm you as much as your own thoughts unguarded.'

'You are beautiful as you are'

Being whole does not mean you do not learn or grow or evolve, it is about how you respond to problems because that makes a difference in who you are. So many of us hide our light, we simply do not own ourselves fully. Life is all about self-discovery. Do not be afraid to shine your light on others without dimming someone else's light. I repeat myself, it is not selfish to love yourself. *It is only when you love yourself enough you build the capacity to love others.*

Now think about the worst thing that has ever happened to you. Now pause and see if you can look at the incident as the best thing that could have happened to you because of the insights you gained from that experience. Just thinking along these lines will change your entire perspective to life, and you will begin to see possibilities of growth you would have never imagined. Suffering does not happen the moment an event occurs, suffering happens the way you choose to see it and the stories you tell yourself about it. When you change the story about a bad experience, the suffering ceases to exist.

I vividly remember, the year was 2016 and the place was Nashville. I was waiting in a queue outside a washroom of a restaurant and saw a lady sitting near the washbasin and sobbing uncontrollably and saying aloud, 'The world is evil. Bad things always happen to me. He left me even after everything we had been through. I'm so disgusted.'

Her friend was consoling her and telling her, 'Jennifer, you're beautiful as you are, you don't need anyone else to make you complete. Just because that guy doesn't see your worth doesn't mean you are unworthy. You deserve someone better, someone who loves you for who you are.'

Take nature as your guide

Nature gives us a powerful lesson on being worthy. A mango tree has its own importance and so does a banyan tree. Each serves a different and an important purpose. Similarly, no one can make us complete. Others can complement us, not complete us.

There is no better half...

People often introduce their life partners as their better half. The usual statement that is thrown our way is 'He/She completes me.'

HELL NO!

There is no better half, only bitter half. Kidding!

Why does someone have to be the 'better' half in the relationship? Does that make you the worse half? I sure hope not! A flourishing relationship is less about two halves and more about two 'wholes'. Your life partner can complement you or enhance your life, but no one completes you because the other person is a whole person and so are *you*. You are complete as you are.

When you embrace both parts of yourself—the good and the bad— you become whole.

Self-esteem and you

Nathaniel Branden's pioneering work in the field of self-esteem is well-known. He defines self-esteem as 'the experience of being competent to cope with the basic challenges of life and of being worthy of happiness'. In his bestselling book *The Six Pillars of Self-esteem*, Dr Braden mentions six practices that are essential for nurturing and sustaining healthy self-esteem and they are:

1. The practice of living consciously

2. The practice of self-acceptance

3. The practice of self-responsibility

4. The practice of self-assertiveness

5. The practice of purposefulness

6. The practice of integrity.[2]

What is wrong with the 'Self-esteem Movement'?

The problem with the narrative of the self-esteem movement in social media is encouraging people to be positive all the time, now that is an unrealistic way of conducting oneself. I am not in favour of blindly chanting positive affirmations like, I am special, I love my body, I can do everything, several times a day. Unless you do not commit to taking actions on your affirmations, they will not work for you.

There are days when I do not feel positive about myself and feel unhappy with the way I am pursuing certain tasks. Maybe I am procrastinating because a big, fat pimple suddenly popped up on my face when I have a presentation to give. What is needed in that moment is to embrace those feelings and reassure myself that these minor issues do not make me unworthy or incomplete. Avoid nursing low self-esteem at all cost because 'it's like driving through life with the handbrake on' (Maxwell Maltz).

Being your own BFF

Self-love involves treating yourself the way you would treat your best friend when they are having a tough time. Learn to be a good, supportive friend to yourself in moments of

2. Nathaniel Branden, 'Preface to Self-Esteem at Work', 2013, https://nathanielbranden.com/project/preface-to-selfesteem-at-work/, accessed on 22 September 2022.

self-doubt, anxiety, sadness and confusion. *Your personality is not fixed, it is dynamic.*

Self-belief is crucial for self-motivation. When you have unconditional self-worth, the approval of others is inconsequential. At the same time, there will be days you feel a bit low and are unable to see your own light or greatness, do not hesitate to reach out for help from people in your safe space. When I am going through a very hard time, I give myself a little TLC (tender, loving, care) that I need.

Do not only focus on the 'hole' in the whole. You are worthy and whole as you are. The person you are today is a result of your life experiences. There have been defining moments, situations, people and events that have shaped you into the person you are today. Who you are today is also a result of the stories you have told yourself about what happened to you in the past.

His Holiness, the 14th Dalai Lama encapsulated this idea beautifully, 'Having compassion for oneself is the basis for developing compassion for others.'

Break free from the prison of conditioning.

So the million-dollar question is 'How do you improve your relationship with yourself?'

Well, by being brutally honest with yourself and asking yourself, what kind of person are you really and how can you change the age-old narrative to the new narrative about yourself.

Think of incidents from your life and build a new narrative for yourself.

I used to see myself as   to   I *choose* to now see myself as

....

....

....

You would begin to notice that all your feelings and behavioural patterns are always in alignment with how you view yourself. If you think you are lazy, you will find a way to be lazy in spite of all your good intentions to break free from the mould because you would justify by saying, 'This is who I am.' Rubbish!

If I challenge this narrative and ask you to think of instances where you submitted a project on time by burning the midnight oil, you will be unable to deny it. This clearly means you have it in you to do it, just the label (or for that matter the perception) needs to change.

Take another example, your friend may consider themselves to be commitment-phobic and offer that as an explanation for all their short and disastrous romantic liaisons. Harbouring such kind of a negative self-image reflects lack of introspection. You can easily change your self-image. And the reason is simple: You are more powerful than you think. Be mindful of how you talk to yourself because you are listening. The moment you begin to see yourself as whole, others too will see you as whole.

Be kind to your younger self that did not know the things you know now. Love yourself. You do not need external validation. There is no one else on this planet like you. *Every little thing of you makes you unique, magnificent and whole.*

Think of an incident <u>where you were harsh on yourself</u>. If you were to offer an advice as your best friend, what would you say to yourself?

....

....

....

....

....

....

....

....

....

....

3

UNTIE THE KNOTS OF YOUR MIND

Break Free

'None but ourselves can free our minds.'

—Bob Marley

Over a weekend, my husband, Vikas, and I took a trip to a temple at the top of a hill, which required us to climb quite a few rocky steps. We were twenty-five minutes into the climb when both of us were feeling exhausted.

'Just about fifty more steps, Ma'am, and we will reach the temple,' said our tour guide.

I gasped instantly.

Even after climbing hundred odd steps, we had not reached the top. Just the thought of climbing fifty more was making me exhausted. I kept gasping for air, as I tried to get my legs to stop shaking.

'Oh great! Just fifty more steps. Let's do this,' said Vikas.

But as he turned to look at me we both were confused seeing each other's reactions. I could not fathom how he could expect me to be excited when our bodies were giving up on us. Clearly, Vikas was on a different tangent.

I was amazed to see how two people can approach the same situation in two completely different ways. In other words, both of us were operating from different sets of mental models.

Did you know that every decision any human being makes is made at least *twice*? Let me explain.

A decision is first made in your mind before it is ever made in reality. Remember the time when you were to meet a friend to discuss an issue? Before meeting your friend, you must have played the impending conversation in your mind. And when you finally meet the friend, you end up expressing exactly those thoughts. What determined the outcome? The answer is your underlying belief system about the situation. For instance, if you were operating from a belief of one-upmanship, then your actions will be guided by thoughts and feelings wanting to show how superior you are. In the end, through a self-fulfilling prophecy, you would have turned the discussion into a win–lose argument.

Your beliefs are a result of your mental models that generate thoughts in your mind, which create feelings inside you, which ultimately influence your actions.

MENTAL MODEL STIMULUS → THOUGHTS → FEELINGS → ACTIONS

Mental model: know your mental toolbox

A mental model is the shortcut your brain takes to assess a situation and make a decision. These are the stories and explanations you tell yourself about what is happening around you. During your journey of life, you must have gathered a lot of experiences. And you, like all of us, have built a repository of beliefs and ideas that you rely on to make your everyday decisions. These mental models shape the way you think, help you to simplify complex information and make decisions.

You perceive and interpret the world around yourself through your mental models. They include perceptions, assumptions and beliefs you carry in your mind about how the world works. Look at them like the toolbox for life, remember the bigger your toolbox, the better is your ability to solve problems, make better decisions and think more creatively.

The term 'Mental Model' was coined by Kenneth Craik in his book *The Nature of Explanation* (1943). Later, many researchers did immense work on this topic including Jay Wright Forrester who defined mental model as 'The image of the world around us, which we carry in our head, is just a model. You can discover a solution to a problem if you believe you can and you will not find a solution if you believe you can't.'

You do not even realise that the accumulation of years and years of conditioning in your mind have led you to think, believe and act in a particular way, and you begin to see the world around you in a certain manner through that lens of conditioning.

How do your mental models play out in your life?

Let us do an exercise. I want you to visualise who comes to your mind, the moment you hear the following words:

- Gynaecologist
- Biker
- Author

Was the gynaecologist a man? Was the biker a woman? And who was the author? (Someone like me?) Your answers will depend upon your conditioning.

Your brain creates an image of what seems familiar and discards the unfamiliar, creating an unconscious bias. The unconscious biases influence your judgements or behaviour towards yourself and others. Your actions represent the tip of an iceberg. And your unconscious biases are below the surface of the ocean that you are not mindful of.

One of the most critical steps in expanding your mental models is to be aware of the fact that there is a very real chance that you are not seeing the whole picture of any situation. This gives you a chance to step back, and take a broader look at the available facts/evidences in any given situation. At the end, you take decisions based on your beliefs—the choice lies with you. Do you want that to be a narrow belief or a broad one?

The choice is yours. After all, 'A mind is like a parachute. It doesn't work if it is not open (Frank Zappa).'

Do not be *that* elephant

Let me share a popular anecdote that my father shared with me when I was contemplating a job change early in my career in 2003. I was feeling anxious about navigating the change and here is what he narrated to boost my morale.

This story makes a powerful example of how mental models shape our perceptions.

Shyam saw a baby elephant tied to a small, thin rope to its front leg at his neighbour's house. He has been observing this elephant being tied to the rope wound around a tree for a long time and was very confused about why it did not make an attempt to free itself. Given its size and strength, the elephant could easily tear this rope, but for some reason did not. Shyam could not hold his curiosity any more and went up to his neighbour to find out the reason behind the elephant's rather strange behaviour.

The neighbour said, 'Well, when the elephant was younger, we used the exact same size and type of rope to tie him. He did try to break free then but couldn't because he was not strong enough to break it. When he grew up, he conditioned his mind to believe that no matter how much he tried, he will never break free. And he still believes that the rope can hold him, so he never tries to break free.'

This story made me think. I could relate to it at so many different levels. It helped me realise that my mental rope of thoughts was tying me down and not helping me pursue my goals. I had programmed myself to think that if I were to make a job change, I will lose my credibility and relationships that I had nurtured over the years. I had no real evidence of this assumption, I simply believed it to be true. Just like the baby elephant, I could tell that this rope will keep getting stronger, limiting me even more.

My father helped me realise how I was, like many others, simply unable to look beyond my conditioning. He concluded with the following advice, which has held me in good stead: 'Nancy you are not stuck, you are simply conditioned to follow certain beliefs because they served you in the past, but you can now come to terms with the idea that they might not serve you in the present.' He added that we need to know that we have the power to change our imagination to something more fulfilling and turn it into reality.

How many times have you found yourself stuck in a situation with no way out? You are not the only *one*. You too like the rest are all bound by your mental ropes from which you need to break free. It is only then that you can move in the direction of becoming free.

A deep dive into mental models

Imagine this for a moment: you are watching news on TV when the news anchor says, 'Breaking News: The world is in sheer chaos and the entire economy is under recession.' You then switch to another channel, where someone is interviewing an entrepreneur who raised 200 million dollars of investment and witnessed 150 per cent growth in their organisation. The interviewer ends the interview with the following conclusion: 'We are seeing immense improvement in the market and we are happy to welcome good times ahead.'

And now you are sitting with a huge question mark on your face, as you hear the two absolutely conflicting views about the economy. At this point, you will believe the 'news' based on your mental models.

Do you want to make decisions based on your unconscious bias without clear reasoning, or do you want to make well-informed decisions?

I know it is a rhetorical question, but it is important to reflect upon it.

All movement (thinking) first begins in the mind before any movement happens in the outside world (action). Whether or not you are conscious, your inner talk is at play most of the time even while you are reading these lines, your mind is in full processing mode.

There must be many thoughts running through your mind to help you make sense of what you are reading. *Is this true? Is what she is saying useful? Should I skip reading a few lines?* These thoughts run on an autopilot mode without any effort on your part, and that, my friend, is your mental model at play.

And sometimes, your mental models could disempower you and prevent you from living a gratifying life because they advance your negative assumptions in play and do not support you in making correct decisions.

Yes, you can re-wire your brain

According to a research, human beings are exposed to around eleven million bits of information per second and our conscious brain has the capacity to process around fifty bits per second.[1]

We are bombarded with a million pieces of information every day and it is humanly impossible to assess each and every one that comes our way and hence we form decisions based on our experiences, or what we believe is the mindful valuation of a situation.

---

1. Encyclopedia Britannica, 'Physiology', https://www.britannica.com/science/information-theory/Physiology, accessed on 27 May 2022.

Once you are aware of your mental models, you will learn to assess a situation from a multi-dimensional perspective and avoid taking decisions based on your own biases. This awareness will not only give you the power to make informed decisions, but also help you understand why some people behave the way they do.

'One of the greatest fictions of all is to deny the complexity of the world and think in absolute terms.' Yuval Noah Harari could not have been more right.

And if you continue to look at a problem or a situation in a biased way, you might ignore blind spots and create false dichotomies, which will impair your decision-making ability.

In 2013, Daniel Gregory Amen, an American psychiatrist, in his TEDx talk spoke about the intersection of medical imaging and psychiatry. He said, 'So after 22 years and 83,000 brain scans, the single most important lesson my colleagues and I have learned is that you can *literally* change people's brains. And when you do, you change their life.'[2]

Yes, mental models are not fixed and you can rebuild your mental muscle and improve your life. In the next few paragraphs, I have provided some examples and references on the power that mental models possess.

---

2. Daniel Amen, 'The Most Important Lesson From 83,000 Brain Scans', New World Artificial Intelligence, 26 February 2021, https://www.newworldai.com/the-most-important-lesson-from-83-000-brain-scans-daniel-amen/, accessed on 27 May 2022.

Smartphone applications frequently release updates to fix bugs, ensure the app's functioning is more stable and release new features to improve customer experience. It is the user who has the power to decide whether or not they want to opt for these updates. Majority of us opt for software updates for enhanced experience. Isn't it? If you carry the old software everywhere without the right updates, it is bound to cause you problems.

Now, the question that you need to ask yourself is, *When was the last time I upgraded myself?*

Okay, time for some exercise! Relax. Mental, not physical.

Deconstruct your life

Let us do an exercise.

Ask yourself: *What are your mental models regarding your building blocks of life?* Try not to give the correct answer just focus on providing an honest one.

What is a must-have for you in a relationship?

How would you describe your health condition?

What is your relationship with money?

What gives you job satisfaction?

The way you see the world around you can either help you move closer towards joy and create mental freedom, or move you towards pain and build a mental prison for yourself.

'After all, the world is nothing but your own magnified mind.' (Osho)

Are you a prisoner of your mind?

I am sure you have met that one person who thinks that they are taken for granted by everyone and that the world is unkind to them. They go around carrying a mental model of victimhood. They believe that something outside of themselves is causing problems in their lives. An alternative way of thinking is to pause and analyse your mental models or biases. Every thought of yours, whether positive or negative, grows stronger with constant repetition.

When you harbour thoughts like —I am *not* a creative person, I *cannot* draw, I hate *socialising*—you give yourself labels and the problem with these labels is that they are limiting.

Which thoughts do you tell yourself repeatedly? Are they helping you or harming you to lead your life? Which labels have you given yourself to define your identity? Please list them down.

_____

_____

_____

_____

_____

How to break free...

Do not become a prisoner of your mind. Because you may be caught in the trap. In his brilliant book, *A New Earth: Awakening to Your Life's Purpose*, Eckhart Tolle says beautifully, 'Thinking without awareness is the main dilemma of human existence.'

This does not mean that you need to scrutinise every thought because that would just be impractical and exhausting. Dr Joseph Murphy explains this well in his book *Believe in Yourself*: '[Y]ou should know that you are the master of your own thoughts and all these thoughts are nothing but your mental chatter and you can challenge them and make a different choice instead.' Simply recognising this will expand your mental horizon. Because as someone once said, 'When things change inside you, things change around you.'

The added bonus of raising your awareness on your mental models is that you also gain insight into why people behave the way they do. The best way to work with mental models is to turn the mirror inwards and reflect on what are the alternative ways of thinking about the same beliefs. This will help you to expand your thinking and create a better reality for yourself.

How do you hold your identity in your mind? That is your mental model of how you view yourself. This reminds me of one of my favourite quotes from *Hamlet*: 'There is nothing either good or bad, but thinking makes it so.'

Speaking of Shakespeare, in one of his most recognisable plays, *The Merchant of Venice* this issue is tackled with élan. Right in the opening scene, we find one of the lead characters, Antonio, express his melancholy to his peers. When each one of his pals tries to identify the reason behind his sadness, he refutes them all and says, 'I hold the world but as the world; Gratiano, a stage where every man must play a part, and mine a sad one.'

Gratiano, his friend, replies, 'Well then, let me play the fool: With mirth and laughter let old wrinkles come.'

If you look at the world in the way Antonio did, you might end up feeling distressed. Instead, it is important to identify where such a notion is stemming from in the first place. What Gratiano says provides a good insight into his mental model.

It is important to acknowledge and confront your flawed thinking because it will stop you from functioning to your optimal capacity. Developing your mind by becoming aware of these biases will help you to make more informed choices in life.

Seven biases that hamper your growth

Let me explain this further. Sometimes your own beliefs are like a mirage. Every single decision you make in life is not always based on how things are but rather, how *you believe them to be*. This is what is known as unconscious bias.

Unconscious bias or implicit bias was first introduced in a 2006 paper by the social scientist Anthony Greenwald. The researcher's work has shown how much implicit bias can shape social behaviour and decision-making.

To quote from an article which articulates this well: 'Even people with the best intentions are influenced by these hidden attitudes, behaving in ways that can create disparities in hiring practices, student evaluations, law enforcement, criminal proceedings—pretty much anywhere people are making decisions that affect others. Such disparities can result from bias against certain groups, or favoritism toward other ones. Today, implicit bias is widely understood to be a cause of unintended discrimination that leads to racial, ethnic, socioeconomic and other inequalities.'[3]

Implicit bias often leads us to making incorrect decisions or arriving at incorrect conclusions. Avoiding these biases can help us in solving problems and making better decisions. You need to challenge them to expand your horizon. The way to let go of such beliefs is to ask yourself:

Is this belief serving me or harming me?

What does it still give me that I am not letting go of it?

What options have I not considered? Or, for that matter what options do I need to consider?

---

3. Betsy Mason, 'Curbing Implicit Bias: What Works And What Doesn't', Discover, https://knowablemagazine.org/article/mind/2020/how-to-curb-implicit-bias., accessed on 28 May 2022.

There are many unconscious biases, but I will discuss the seven common ones that hamper our personal growth:[4]

Negativity bias

Have you noticed that criticism has a far deeper impact on you than compliments? No, you are not the only one. That is why it takes years for some people to forget traumatic experiences while small, joyful moments quickly turn into distant memories. This is because our brain is wired to absorb negative news faster than positive one. Psychologists refer to this as negativity bias. The news channels are aware of this and they use it to manipulate their audience. This tendency to register negative information more readily than positive information can have a deep impact on your behaviour, decisions, relationships, etc.

Strategy to follow: Enhance your self-awareness and focus on positive thinking. Whenever you find yourself indulging in negative self-talk ask yourself: *What is the alternative or a more balanced thought*? As the famous artist Andy Warhol once observed, 'Don't pay any attention to what they write about you. Just measure it in inches.' In other words, it does not matter what people say about you or how much they talk about you—they are still thinking about you by giving you importance.

4. Wikipedia. 'List of cognitive biases', 20 September 2022, https://en.wikipedia.org/wiki/List_of_cognitive_biases, accessed on 23 September 2022.

A word of caution here, do not fall into the trap of pseudo positivity. Be optimistic but realistic at the same time. 'Realistic optimists believe they will succeed, but also believe they have to *make success happen* through efforts, careful planning, persistence and choosing the right strategies. They recognise the need for giving serious thought to how they will deal with obstacles.'[5]

Status quo bias

The term 'status quo bias' was introduced by researchers William Samuelson and Richard Zeckhauser in 1988. As the name suggests, people operating from this bias prefer that things stay as they are or that the current state of affairs remains the same. They fear change and prefer to stay in their comfort zone. Change can be scary for people who prefer to let situations be as they are. If you suffer from this bias then it can have an adverse effect on not only your personal growth, but also your financial status, health, relationships and other significant aspects of your life. Because 'no matter who you are, no matter what you did, no matter where you've come from, you can always change, become a better version of yourself,' as Madonna wisely put once.

Strategy to follow: You can overcome this bias by initiating small changes and then slowly expanding your appetite to

---

5. Heidi Grant, 'Be an Optimist Without Being a Fool', Harvard Business Review, 2 May 2011, https://hbr.org/2011/05/be-an-optimist-without-being a#:~:text=Realistic%20optimists%20(the%20kind%20Bandura,they%20will%20deal%20with%20obstacles, accessed on 22 September 2022.

take big risks because this will build your risk-taking muscle and small micro wins will eventually lead to macro wins in your life.

Scarcity Mindset

A scarcity mindset is when you are so obsessed with a lack of something—usually time or money—that you cannot seem to focus on anything else, no matter how hard you try. Scarcity mentality is not something you do on purpose. It is the background noise your brain makes when you cannot get what you want. But it will cost you.'[6]

Strategy to follow: You need to work on building an abundance mindset by:

- focusing on what you have,
- practising gratitude and
- surrounding yourself with positive people.

Enough is a feast as one Buddhist proverb goes. Reflect upon it.

Confirmation bias

Your socio-cultural background, conditioning, upbringing, etc., impact your beliefs. Some people tend to only seek out information that matches with their pre-existing viewpoints

6. Dan Brennan, 'What Is Scarcity Mentality', WebMd, 25 October 2021, https://www.webmd.com/mental-health/what-is-scarcity-mentality#:~:text=A%20scarcity%20mindset%20is%20when,matter%20how%20hard%20you%20try, accessed on 28 May 2022.

and beliefs, while ignoring information that goes against their beliefs. This is called confirmation bias. If you count yourself among them, then such resistance and adherence to old beliefs could cloud your judgement and decision-making. The more comfortable you are with something, the more likely you are to go on an autopilot mode and that increases the chances of making biased decisions. For example, Sameer believes that all women are bad drivers. He tends to look for evidence to support his argument and ignores evidence that proves that women can also be good drivers. His main assumption will drive his conversation and hamper his ability to be open to other viewpoints.

Strategy to follow: Gather a fair balance of information to obtain an objective view of any given situation. Always weigh all alternative views and options before making a critical decision.

Social Proof Bias

If you have the tendency to follow the herd, then you suffer from social proof bias or the bandwagon effect.

This behaviour is due to the desire to fit in. I understand. You do not want to feel left out and following what the majority of people are doing becomes part of your survival strategy. You need to understand that just because something is popular it does not necessarily mean that you need to do it. Stop following trends blindly because you are unique with unique wants and needs.

Strategy to follow: Stick to your views when you have strong faith in them, especially when they are right, even if others may not follow them. Remember, 'The one thing that doesn't abide by majority rule is a person's conscience.' As Atticus Finch, literature's one of the most popular characters, famously said in Harper Lee's Pulitzer-Prize-winning novel, *To Kill a Mockingbird*. History has shown that people who changed the world were the ones who were initially doubted by others, but it was their self-belief that changed people's perception over time. People who have changed the world were not followers but leaders—Netaji Subhash Chandra Bose, Abraham Lincoln, Nelson Mandela to name a few.

Sunk cost fallacy

Sometimes when you have invested a lot of time and effort into something (be it in a relationship or a project), you continue to invest in it even if it is leading nowhere. It is because you believe your efforts will pay off sooner or later, as you have already invested so much of time, money and effort. This is the reason why many people continue to stay in toxic relationships.

Strategy to follow: If a certain relationship is not working ask yourself: *What is the story you are telling yourself about it working in the future?*

You need to understand that carrying a meaningless relationship or a venture will be more painful to you in the long run.

Victim mindset

If you operate from a victim mindset, you believe all bad things will happen to you and blame others for what you are feeling or experiencing. You can grow emotionally only when you understand that you are ultimately in control of your emotional responses. No one is coming to save you; you have to save yourself from your own thoughts that are not empowering you.

Strategy to follow: Take responsibility for your own actions and realise that only you have a choice of how you look at a situation. 'If you act like a victim, you are likely to be treated as one.' (Paulo Coelho)

Seven popular mental model frameworks to create a mental shift

I will now look at the other side of the coin and share seven popular mental models that have had a positive influence on my thinking. Each mental model explores a different perspective on life. As you read these, reflect on each one of them to understand how they apply to the ways you think and make decisions. A deep understanding of these models will help you to expand your awareness and will come in handy as a toolbox when you are looking to test assumptions and make an informed and intentional choice.

Building awareness around your mental models and frameworks is similar to a mechanic carrying a toolbox with him when they visit someone's place to fix things. He carries his entire toolbox so that he can make use of a particular tool that will best serve the purpose in that given situation.

10/10/10

Most of us have the tendency to take decisions with a short-term view without realising the impact of that decision in the long term. Such decisions are generally in the grip of visceral emotions like anger, lust, anxiety, greed. We all do that. But do not be a slave to your emotions. And no, sleeping on it is not enough. What you need is a strategy. One tool that you can use was invented by Suzy Welch, a business writer. It is called 10/10/10.[7]

The 10/10/10 framework encourages you to ask yourself a few critical questions that help you understand the impact of the choice you decide to make in 10 minutes, 10 months and 10 years.

For instance, when you are eating junk food excessively, ask yourself how you will feel ten minutes after binging. You might say to yourself, *Oh, it's perfectly fine*. But then I would request you to pause and ask how you will feel in ten months if you continue to consume junk food like this. And then, how will you feel after ten years of making this choice? Not asking these questions will block

---

7. Chip Heath and Dan Heath, 'The 10/10/10 Rule For Tough Decisions', FastCompany, 1 April, https://www.fastcompany.com/3007613/10-10-10-rule-tough-decisions, accessed on 30 May 2022.

you from seeing the adverse impact your impulsive or rash decisions will make in the long run just for a momentary gain.

Okay, okay. I understand binging after a heartbreak or at a reunion or a college party, but this cannot become a habit. Why? Because the repercussions are grave. As Anthony Liccione rightly said, 'Hit the bottom and get back up; or hit the bottle and stay down.'

Think of any aspect of your life you are struggling with, whether it is exercising regularly or building a new habit and use the 10/10/10 model to reshape your thinking. When you get into the habit of thinking of long-term consequences, you will overcome any doubts that you might have.

Inverted thinking

Inversion is the practice of solving a problem in reverse. It helps you to turn the problem on its head, break your existing assumptions and as a result reflect on possibilities that you would normally not consider. So, instead of asking yourself (as usual), *What can I do to achieve this outcome and how can I succeed in a particular situation*? You will now begin to ask yourself: *What behaviours or actions can prevent me from solving this problem or achieving the desirable outcome*? You will be able to resolve many difficult problems when you look for a solution this way.

'Inversion is a powerful thinking tool because it puts a spotlight on errors and roadblocks that are not obvious at first glance.'[8] (James Clear) For instance, when you are launching a new product or service, ask yourself: *What would prevent people from buying the product?*

The more you understand the pitfalls of making a decision, the better equipped you will be to make informed decisions.

Building internal locus of control

This framework was developed by American psychologist Julian B. Rotter in 1954, and has since become an aspect of personality psychology. He shared that an individual's locus of control can be internal or external. Your locus of control can influence how you respond to situations/challenges/problems in your life. 'It is the degree to which the individual interprets events as being a result of their own actions or external factors.'[9]

People with strong internal locus feel confident in the face of challenges whereas people with external locus of control tend to blame or praise external factors for what happens to them and feel powerless in the face of challenging situations. For instance, when you are looking for a job, and if you are someone who leaves it up to fate to get an interview call from someone, you are operating from an external locus of control, whereas if you have faith in your abilities and you reach out and apply at various places, you have a strong internal locus of control.

---

8. James Clear, 'Inversion: The Crucial Thinking Skill Nobody Ever Taught You', https://jamesclear.com/inversion, accessed on 30 May 2022.
9. 'Seeing reality as it is: Why having an internal locus of control is important', Harvard University, 20 November 2008, https://blogs.harvard.edu/sammy/2008/11/20/internal-locus-of-control/, accessed on 3 September 2022.

A person with internal locus of control takes ownership and accountability for their life.

Regret minimisation framework

This is the framework Jeff Bezos used when he had to make an important decision about Amazon. In a *60 Minutes* interview, from 1997, Jeff Bezos said, 'I want to have lived my life in such a way that when I'm 80 years old I've minimized the number of regrets that I have.'

Thus, when the journalist highlighted, that was not exactly a 'carpe diem' moment (a moment driven by instinct, rather than reason) Jeff Bezos explained, 'I don't go in for carpe diem, I go in for regret minimization framework!'[10]

PICK and HATS frameworks

When you are making critical decisions, follow the PICK framework:

Pause,

Inspect bias,

Curious and

Kind

---

10. Gennaro Cuofano, 'Regret Minimization Framework In A Nutshell', FourWeek MBA, 23 June, https://fourweekmba.com/regret-minimization-framework/, accessed on 30 August 2022.

Whenever you are in the middle of a crisis, pause for a few seconds, then inspect if there are any biases at play that can hamper your decision-making. If you are unable to clearly see the complete picture, be curious enough to ask others and test your assumptions to gain a good perspective of the situation in hand. And most importantly, be kind to yourself and others when you finally make the decision.

HATS: This is interpreted as whenever I am **h**ungry, **a**ngry, **t**ired or **s**cared, I must avoid making an important decision in that moment.

Antonio R. Demasio, David Dornsife, Professor of Neuroscience, University of Southern California said, 'We are not thinking machines that feel. We are feeling machines that think.' Your brain can easily be clouded by emotions, hence taking a step back, delaying taking decisions in critical situations can help you to make informed decisions.

Identity shift and alternate reality

James Clear in his bestselling book, *Atomic Habits*, talks about the best way to change behaviour. He suggests not to struggle to change a habit, instead *change your identity*. Focus on gaining a new identity. For instance, if you want to be the person who goes to gym thrice a week, you should focus on building a new identity of a person who has a body of an athlete.

Pick any situation from your life that is of concern to you and in which you want to see a shift. Visualise the desired situation in detail and then construct an alternate reality that is better than your current reality. This visualisation exercise will create an inner shift in you and help you to move towards an alternate reality, which will help you to maximise your potential.

Pareto Principle

The Pareto Principle or 80/20 rule was introduced in 1906 by Italian economist Vilfredo Pareto.[11] The principle states that 80 per cent of the results you get out of something comes from 20 per cent of the causes. For example, have you noticed you wear 20 per cent of your favourite clothes 80 per cent of the time? 80 per cent of the business of many organisations comes from their top 20 per cent clients. Researchers also call it the secret framework of achieving more with less.

Reality is made of zigzag lines, not straight lines

Whatever you have learnt about mental models so far will only make sense if you diagnose your situations and widen your thinking lens and ask yourself: *What do I need to know that I don't know while making decisions?* Our mental models are like an *invisible rule book* that we carry in our mind to make sense of the world and we must use them for our benefit. All these laws exist in our mind, and the evaluator inside us bases everything on these rules.

---

11. Kevin Kruse, 'The 80/20 Rule And How It Can Change Your Life', Forbes, 7 March 2016, https://www.forbes.com/sites/kevinkruse/2016/03/07/80-20-rule/?sh=50751f923814, accessed on 4 September 2022.

All personal breakthroughs begin with a change in beliefs. How do you replace your limiting beliefs? The most effective way is to destabilise your old belief and to shake your certainty by questioning it.

Ask yourself and make a note:

What beliefs do I hold strongly about how the world functions?

_____

_____

_____

What beliefs do I carry about how love, marriage and relationships should function?

_____

_____

_____

What have my beliefs cost me? How have they limited me in the past?

_____

_____

_____

What could it cost me in the future if I do not change now?

_____

_____

_____

How to transition to new mental models

There is enough evidence in science that you can train your brain to build new neural pathways. This is known as neuroplasticity. Our brain has the ability to rewire itself. Its restructures are based on the changes we consciously make in our thoughts and behaviours. Again, whatever we are not changing, *we are choosing*.

R. Buckminster Fuller, architect, philosopher and futurist, said it beautifully, 'You never change things by fighting the existing reality. To change something, build a new model that makes the existing model obsolete.'

The more self-aware you become of your mental models, the more aware you will become of thoughts that serve you and the ones you need to discard or challenge.

Remember, *you are the number one agent of change in your life*. Reprogramming your mind is one of the best gifts you can give to yourself. What you can learn, you can unlearn too by being curious about new things.

'I am neither especially clever, nor especially gifted. I am only very, very curious.' (Albert Einstein)

We all operate from biases and certain mental models. In order to come up with new ideas, you need to not only think differently, but also start seeing things differently.

Just as you exercise your muscles to become stronger, in the same way, through focus and practice you can modify and strengthen your mindset and bounce back from setbacks and challenges that come your way. Your mental models are your most important assets and managing them efficiently will help you approach a problem or a situation from a different perspective and help you be more efficient in decision-making. You must have often heard the idiom 'think outside the box', expanding your mental models helps you to do exactly that.

Remember, it is never too late to start over and change the outdated beliefs that have held you back for so long. Leave your excess baggage and use a new suitcase loaded with empowering mental models that will help you lead an extraordinary life.

The following saying attributed to an ancient Chinese philosopher beautifully captures how the quality of our thoughts shape our lives—Watch your thoughts, they become your words; watch your words, they become your actions; watch your actions, they become your habits; watch your habits, they become your character; watch your character, it becomes your destiny.

Each one of us has got limits and limits are not technical, tactical or physical, they are mostly mental.

List your limiting beliefs and think about the mental models you can use to push them out.

....

....

....

....

....

....

....

....

....

....

4

LIVE BY YOUR VALUES

Your Driving Force

'It's not hard to make decisions, once you know what your values are.'

— Roy E. Disney

If you gave me your debit/credit card statements and your daily schedule of how you spend your day, I could tell you what your values and priorities in life are and who you are as a person. Every choice you make is a depiction of where you would like to invest your time and money and what you value as a person.

Even your most basic decisions are a reflection of your values. For instance, if you value sense of security, it is likely that you may decline any opportunity where you have to undertake high risks because you value being safe and stable much more.

Take another example, let us say your friend told you that you need to be more aggressive in your business dealings with difficult customers. For you, being aggressive means being pushy and being pushy violates your core value of compassion and hence you ignored the advice.

If you are someone who values honesty, you will call out the wrongdoings of others. Your values reflect in your behaviour unconsciously.

Whatever crucial decisions you have made in your life till date have led you to where you are today. As easy as it is to shift the blame of your decisions to external factors, it is important to take ownership for your choices and their consequences because ultimately you are responsible for your own life.

Values are reflected not so much in what we say we love doing, it is reflected in what you eventually *end up* doing.

Values are the principles or standards you set for your own behaviour, they represent your unique essence. Values are the personal qualities you choose to follow, to guide your actions and lead your life with purpose. It is important and critical to know your values because they build your self-awareness and make you a more confident person. Above all, you are able to communicate assertively with others, lead a peaceful life sans unnecessary stress.

Are your everyday decisions in alignment with what you value? If not, then knowing your personal core values can help you do exactly that.

When you know what is important to you, it is easy for you to stop focusing your energy on things that are futile and instead invest your time, energy and money on doing things that matters the most to you.

Have you ever wondered why you like to do certain things and avoid doing other things—the answer lies in your core values.

We all face challenges in life and a critical part of being effective is to know what is important to you in a given situation, what is at stake for you and what would it mean if you do not get it? The better you know yourself through your values, the better position you will be in to lead a life with purpose and fulfilment.

Your core values: the Whys, Whats and Hows of your life

'Don't let the noise of others' opinions drown out your own inner voice.' (Steve Jobs)

Your core values are your guiding principles. When you are in the middle of making a critical decision, it is your values that guide you in deciding—what to say yes to and what to say no to. They are your inner compass that guides you through the choices and decisions you make in life.

There are people who spend every day of their lives doing what they love doing and look forward to each day and then there are others who do not quite know where they are headed. People in the first category lead their lives with an understanding of their core values.

Your core values are non-negotiable. Core values like honesty, openness, integrity are not just mere words when you incorporate these in your behaviour and live by them, they determine your destiny.

Core values define your character, who you are and what you are like as a person. Core values are your inner essence. They are the 'Whys' behind all the 'Whats' and 'Hows' of your life decisions.

Find anchor in your core values

Life can be challenging, you will face failures, setbacks, things that do not go the way you want; so sometimes, you need something to anchor you, something to hold on to, something that gives you a sense of direction. Knowing your core values and what matters to you will provide that anchor to help you come out of stormy situations where you feel stuck.

And when you operate from your core values, you love what you do and it leads you to a state of flow. You lead your life with authenticity and do not feel the need to hide behind a mask, or pretend to be someone that you are not. You also develop the ability to deeply listen to others, observe what they say and at the same time, come to your own conclusions while having respect for other people's values at the same time but not be defined or bound by their values.

Your core values: the inner GPS

'It's not what happens to us, but our response to what happens to us that hurts us.' (Stephen R. Covey)

And your response depends on your core values. Your core values are your inner guiding direction tool (IGDT). Just like the GPS guides you on the road, your IGDT inspires and guides you to take action in congruence with what you value most. Your values inject fuel in your life. Every day you face a lot of choices and hence making decisions can be an overwhelming experience. The good news is by getting clarity on your core values, you begin to lead a life with purpose by filtering out things that do not matter to you and making decisions based on what is truly important to you. Your values are a window to your soul.

We are all walking repositories of treasure. Just like diamonds are found at a great depth below the surface of the earth your core values are the deep treasures within you, only waiting to be discovered. Take a deep dive into the inner layers of your soul, and you come out shining like a diamond.

Your journey from confusion to clarity

Knowing your values gives you greater levels of clarity and enables you to set your boundaries for things that are unacceptable to you. One of my core values is personal growth. And this guides me to how I spend my day—the kind of conversations I have, the type of work assignments I take up. One question that I often ask myself—is this task that I am putting my energy and efforts into, helping me to grow as a person? The answer helps me to stay connected to my core value of personal growth and keeps me focused on things that I care most about and discard decisions that are not in alignment with my values.

How to make your soul dance

Will Rogers once said, 'Too many people spend money they haven't earned, to buy things they don't want, to impress people they don't like.'

Don't be one of them.

How to ensure that?

Well, answer the question: How do you choose your priorities?

I have tried to look at this question from many different ways, and an effective way that has worked for me is to have a clearly defined values compass to which I can align my decisions. This kind of synchronisation has always helped me to make mindful decisions that I can own in complete harmony with myself. Doing more of what brings you joy, makes your soul do a happy dance is when you know for sure, your core values are at play.

At the crossroads?

Let us say you are at the crossroads with two job offers in hand:

Road Number 1 offers you a higher position, bigger team to manage and frequent travel opportunities, but less time for your family.

Road Number 2 offers you a stable job that you truly find purpose in and with the opportunity to spend more time with your family.

Which road would you walk on? I have faced this dilemma of being unsure about which job role will be a better fit for me. Over the years, I have seen many people around me unsure of the choices they need to make.

Your friend or a well-wisher might say, 'Are you silly? What is there to even think, pick Road 1, that is a great opportunity.'

But is that how you would want to make your life choices? Think about it….

I know big decisions like these are not part of everyday matter, but each day you do have to make so many choices. If you stay consistent with making decisions based on your core values, people around you will be quick to observe what you stand for. *Your stance is your brand*. Your values are your driving force. Connecting to your core values is like having a one-on-one meeting with your authentic self.

How to lead an authentic life

In the 1980s, AIDS became a talking point internationally. It was a frightening disease as doctors were yet to find a cure for it. They still have not. People believed that one could catch the infection from touching someone who had the disease.

In April 1987, at the height of the AIDS epidemic, Princess Diana opened the first unit in London, which was dedicated to treating people with AIDS. During one of her visits to the unit, she shook her hands with an AIDS patient without wearing a glove. And this is what she had to say, 'HIV does not make people dangerous to know. You can shake their hands and give them a hug. Heaven knows they need it.'[1]

Her behaviour was full of empathy and she sent out a strong message to the world that AIDS was not infectious. This is a clear example of Princess Diana leading by her core value—empathy. Princess Diana was a proponent of treating everyone equally and the above example shows that she walked the talk.

A political leader whom I admire and respect is Jacinda Ardern. She has received massive appreciation worldwide for her empathetic style of leadership. She once made a profound statement in one of her interviews, 'One of the criticisms I've faced over the years is that I'm not aggressive enough or assertive enough, or maybe somehow, because I'm empathetic, it means I'm weak. I totally rebel against that. I refuse to believe that you cannot be both compassionate and strong.'[2]

---

1. Ian Green, 'How Princess Diana challenged HIV stigma with every hug', *Terrence Higgins Trust* (blog), 30 June 2021, www.tht.org.uk, accessed on 18 July 2022.
2. BBC News, 'Christchurch Shootings: Ardern Vows Never to Say Gunman's Name', BBC, 19 March 2019, https://www.bbc.com/news/world-asia-47620630, accessed on 19 July 2022.

Jacinda's response to the mass shooting at mosques that happened on 15 March 2019 in Christchurch, New Zealand, brought to the forefront her compassion that was never seen before in any political leader of her stature. Her behaviour displayed her ability to stand in solidarity for people who were grieving for their loved ones. She wore a black head scarf and spoke to Muslim leaders and asked them what they would like her to do. 'He sought many things from his act of terror, but this one was notoriety—that is why you will never hear me mention his name,' Ms Ardern said in an emotional address at New Zealand's parliament.

Jacinda's extraordinary display of empathy in the wake of the Christchurch sets an example for other world leaders. The stories of these people tell us how their values were evident in their actions.

We admire people who stand for what they believe in. What do Sudha Murthy, M.S. Dhoni, Ratan Tata, Oprah Winfrey, Michelle Obama, Anand Mahindra have in common? These people became successful and are known to be people of character as they act according to the values they believe in. They are consistent in their actions for what they stand for. History proves that extraordinary achievers have awareness of their highest values and living by them is the secret of their achievements.

'I want people to remember me as a good person, not as a good cricketer.' (M.S. Dhoni)

This pretty much sums it all.

I remember watching an interview of award-winning actress Anushka Sharma where she mentioned that spending time alone with herself is very important to her and she ensures to take time out no matter how hectic her work schedule is. Anushka added that many people misunderstood her to be arrogant and self-absorbed for doing this. However, alone time is an important value to her and when she stayed true to it, slowly people around her started to understand and respect that value.

Many icons in various parts of the world show us how to lead authentic lives with values. You do not have to ape them, you need to be motivated enough to discover what is most important to you and lead your life accordingly. Each person can hold different core values dear to them and lead their lives keeping in mind those core values.

'Values are like fingerprints. Nobody's are the same but you leave them all over everything you do.' (Elvis Presley)

The Jack Sparrow and Elizabeth Swann dilemma

One of my favourite dialogues from *Pirates of the Caribbean* is where Jack Sparrow tells Elizabeth Swann, 'We are very much alike, you and I, I and you…us.'

Elizabeth responds with a smile, 'Oh…except for a sense of honour and decency and a moral centre and personal hygiene.'

A close friend may seem to be just like you, but the things your friend or near one holds dear in life could be totally different from what you hold.

In situations when you feel you are right, but someone else feels you are wrong, do you take a pause to ponder if the other person also might have a meaningful stance? What helps in such situations is to remind yourself that there are two people holding two different values. When you are looking at the same thing differently from the other person because both of you value different things in a given situation and if you want that situation to be cordial, you will have to understand what the other person values and in what way can you come to a common ground by understanding the values that are common to both of you. Instead of being threatened by other people's values, you will begin to celebrate them.

What matters the most to you?

Imagine, God forbid, your home catches fire and you have time to save only three objects. Assume that your near and dear ones who live with you are safe. What three things would you choose to save? And why?

This exercise can help shed light on what you consider truly important, and this ties in strongly with your personal core values. For instance, saving something like your smartphone could either show that you value communication or could show an addiction to your phone, whichever way you choose to look at it; and saving something like your wallet could mean that financial security is most important to you.

Who are you?

If I asked you, who you are minus your titles, job description or relationship descriptions—what would you say? Son? Daughter? Wife? Husband? CEO? Manager? But your core values that you stand by and lead your life with define who you truly are from within. *Who are you?* An empathetic soul or someone who values adventures or a curious person?

Values are the energy currency of your life.

When you have to make a crucial decision, your values help you to make that final call. Sometimes your own emotions get in the way of good decision-making, but if you stop to ask yourself: *What do I value most in this situation?* You will be able to come to a clearer and well-thought-out decision.

Values impact your credibility

'Try not to become a man of success, but rather try to become a man of value.' (Albert Einstein)

Values are directly aligned to your credibility. If people see that you are consistent in following your values in all situations, they trust you. Take the example of the industrialist Ratan Tata. What values are displayed by him? Some common answers will be humility, philanthropy, idealism, astute leadership, etc. These are displayed in his demeanour in most interactions. He lives by his values day in and day out.

Value Roadmap and Discovery Exercise

In one of my coaching sessions, Sumit (name changed for privacy), a twenty-four-old startup founder, had a confession to make. He told me that majority of his friends acted strange, selfish and uncooperative towards him. He was confused as to why they showed a lack of respect for him since he expected to be treated better. I asked Sumit to tell me what he valued most in his relationships?

Sumit began to voice out his needs and also why they were important for him. We then did a Value Roadmap Discovery Exercise (discussed in detail in the following section) to understand his values.

One of Sumit's top core values that he discovered through the exercise was 'belonging'. A sense of belonging for Sumit meant to be accepted by others and to feel included. When Sumit felt a sense of belonging in his relationships, he felt fulfilled and when his value of belonging was compromised, he felt disrespected.

Once he got clarity on his values, he was able to tackle the bigger question in his mind: *Do I exhibit the values that I expect from others in a relationship?*

It is much easier for people to respect you and honour your boundaries when they see you lead by example. Sumit noticed that there was a gap between what he expected from others and what he truly practised in his life. He needed to realise that he should first live by those values before he can expect anyone else to live it for him. Reminds me of the famous Michael Jackson song '*Man in the Mirror*':

> I'm starting with the man in the mirror
>
> I'm asking him to change his ways...
>
> If they wanna make the world a better place
>
> Take a look at yourself and then make a change

After a few months, Sumit finally had a chat with his friends about the misunderstandings that had crept into their relationships due to unfulfilled expectations. By sharing his concerns with honesty, his friends got a better understanding of how they could have a harmonious bond. His friends also shared with him the values that they had in common and this frank conversation about discovering each other's needs enabled them to have a healthy and meaningful friendship going forward. This experience further made him realise that he was a bit out of sync with what he expected from others vis-à-vis the behaviour he was displaying. He understood that instead of leading life from outside in, he had to lead life from inside out.

Sharing values is critical to any relationship. But what is extremely critical to check is whether you are living your life by those values?

If you want to lead a more fulfilling life, getting clarity on what matters to you is an important place to start. If you are ready to take the plunge, then do the Value Roadmap

Discovery Exercise with honesty because it will help you to reflect deeper and understand the narrative you hold about your life and the invisible force that has been controlling the decisions you make. The exercise helps you uncover your core values that are seamlessly hidden in your life experiences. Let us identify your core values through a Value Roadmap Exercise, which is a five-step process.

Step 1: Self-reflection

Take an A4-size paper and draw a line to represent a long road (use the image below as a reference). Imagine your journey of life till date as a road. Take a moment to reflect and make a note of significant experiences starting from your childhood till the present day that stands out in your memory. We must excavate the past; we cannot skip this step. Only by understanding your past patterns can you fully understand how they influence your current ways of being. Plot them on the roadmap of your life in the form of high points (meaningful moments) and low points (moments when you felt frustrated, angry). Make a note of as many events and plot all those experiences.

Roadmap of Life

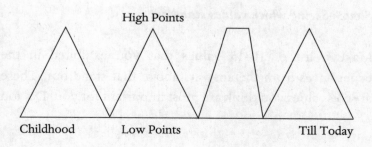

Step 2: Scouting your life journey

After making a note of all the crucial moments of your life, reflect and answer the following questions. Trust me, the journey of answering these questions would be an eye-opener for you.

What do you observe about the high points in your life?

What values were you honouring in those experiences?

Is there a pattern in those high points/experiences?

When you were experiencing low moments or frustration in your life, what values were you compromising or suppressing?

What were you feeling?

If there was an article about you in a newspaper, which of your qualities would be highlighted in it?

On which tasks or activities can you spend hours on end and yet not realise how time flies?

Which value is non-negotiable for you, no matter how strong the temptation is to let go of it?

Step 3: Seeing which values stand out

Make a list of 10–15 values that you exhibited in the experiences from the answers above that stand out. These are the values you think are most important for you. Do you notice certain words that are repeatedly showing in your roadmap in the form of your responses to the questions above? Make a note of it.

Step 4: Sorting and grouping

If you notice certain words, phrases or themes that are similar, group them together. For instance, values like kindness, empathy, compassion can be grouped together. The more a word shows up, the more likely it is to have a powerful connect with you deep within.

Narrow down the 10–15 value words and choose your top 5 values. Rate each value on a scale of 1 to 5, 1 being the least important and 5 being the most important.

Now focus on five core values to simplify your life.

For example:

Value	Rating
Independence	5
Creativity	3

The question that can help you with the rating is: How would I feel if this value is taken away from my life? If you cannot let go of it, that means it is of high value and vice-versa.

Value	Rating (on a scale of 1–5)
....	....
....	....
....	....
....	....
....	....

Step 5: Values missing in action

Once you have identified your core values, it is essential to identify whether these are supporting and empowering you to lead the life you want, or are some of these values holding you back to lead the life that you desire for yourself.

What else is important to you in your life, which has not shown up in the Value Road Map Discovery Exercise?

For example, if your health is important to you, did it show up as a value of high priority, or are you compromising on this value?

If you tell others health is an important value to you but you do not have time to exercise or eat healthy, then this value is not really important to you. Ask yourself:

What is the life you want to create?

What do your values need to be in order to create the life you want?

Identify two values that are not listed and list related actions that you can undertake to inculcate these values in your life.

At different stages of your life, your values might change. Your values need an updation too. Knowing your core values is not enough, you have to live by those values through your actions. Values shape your character. For instance, if compassion is your value, then you ensure you act and live the lesson of this value through your behaviour by treating others with kindness and empathy.

Ask yourself:

What do I really want to experience in life?

How can I focus more of my time and energy on things that will help me create the life I want?

How to strike the diamond mine within yourself

Some of my clients often ask me, 'What if I want to inculcate more values in my life? Is that possible?' My answer is YES. Our values are ever evolving. There are three broad categories of values namely borrowed, authentic and aspirational values.

Borrowed values: These are the values you have imbibed because you were deeply conditioned to do so by your caregivers. These are the values that appeared important for your survival at early stages of your life or that have developed by emulating people you admire without having a deep inner connect with yourself. Imbibing other people's values without having a deep connection with those values is a dangerous path because borrowed values will not help you lead an empowering life.

Authentic values: These are your core values, the ones that helped you make choices in your life, and hence define your character.

Aspirational values: These are values that you admire in others and have a sense that by inculcating these values in your life, you can take your personal self to a higher level and become the best version of yourself.

You strike the diamond mine within yourself when you lead your life with your authentic values. Aspirational values, on the other hand, push you to aspire for an improved version of yourself. It is only when you discover your authentic values, should you strive for aspirational values.

How to live with courage and conviction

Do you recall a time when you were expected to do something that conflicted with what you believed in, but you did it anyway?

Now let us see what you could do if a similar situation arises again. The idea behind this exercise is not to defend your past but to reflect and raise awareness of how you can choose to do things differently in the future.

Consider answering the following questions:

What happened that made it difficult to share what you believed in?

Why did you not speak up and act?

What motivated you to act according to your values?

If you are struggling answering these, consider answering the following questions:

What would make it easier for you to speak up and act?

What is in your control?

What is in another person's control?

What support do you need to make it easy for you?

The power of this self-enquiry is that it highlights what actions you can take that are in your control and what excuses you need to avoid.

Mind the gap

Your actions speak so loudly to the world that people can barely hear what you are saying. And sometimes you find a gap between what you say and what you do. You tell others that your family is important to you, yet you spend the least amount of time with them. You say kindness is important, but you forget to be kind in many instances. You claim, 'I love my parents and I want to call them daily', and still you do not make that call to them. You say fairness is important, yet you kept quiet when someone is treated unfairly. You say to your friend you value your friendship with them but hardly stay in touch with them.

Find your value gaps.

Ask yourself: *Where do I need to bridge the gap between my words and actions?*

Let your values be your guiding light

I do hope that you will now look at your potential differently and spend some time to discover what matters to you most. When you discover your core values, you live a life wholeheartedly. You stop caring about what others think of you.

The more you say no to things that do not matter, the more you can say yes to the ones that do.

Lead a life true to who you are. If you do not give importance to your values, no one else will. Making decisions based on your core values should not be a one-off thing, it should be a daily action.

'Life's no piece of cake, mind you, but the recipe is my own to fool with.' (Haruki Murakami)

On a serious note, when your values and actions do not match, others struggle to trust you. Take the time to align with who you are as a person and what you do.

Let me leave you with some words from Eleanor Roosevelt who summed it up beautifully, 'It's your life—but only if you make it so. The standards by which you live must be your own standards, your own values, your own convictions in regard to what is right and wrong, what is true and false, what is important and what is trivial.'

What do you value most in your life?

....

....

....

....

....

....

....

....

....

....

5

DO NOT BE A MONKEY

Get Your Hand out of the Jar!

'Your relationship to yourself is and always will be directly reflected in all your relationships with others.'

— Vironika Tugaleva

My knotted state of affairs

'Are you Nancy Katyal?'

Asked an elderly lady walking towards me. I instantly stood up from my chair and said, 'Please pardon my memory, but I don't seem to recall if we've met before.'

She told me we were connected through Facebook and that she read my posts often.

'My name is Purnima,' she said.

I smiled and gestured her to sit next to me on the chair.

She asked, 'If I may ask, what brings you to this resort?'

I said, 'Nothing in particular. I just wanted to take a break.'

She immediately responded, 'Break from what?'

'Break from…'

And I paused.

I laughed it off and asked her where she was from and how often she visited the place.

She answered my questions and then added, 'Nancy, at times we feel a bit hesitant to trust a stranger with our emotions though sometimes we need to believe in the process and take a leap of faith by seeking support.'

I reflected on what she said and nodded. Both of us stared at beautiful flowers in front of us.

A few seconds had passed, I do not know why in that moment I felt like I should be open and honest, so I cut the silence and said, 'Purnima, you know that feeling when misunderstandings seep in a friendship that you have nourished for long. You feel like you gave it your all, but the other person appears to take you for a ride every single time. To answer your question, that's exactly why I'm on this break because situations like these make me feel unsettled and emotionally exhausted.'

Purnima listened intently.

'I've had that happen to me too.'

She took out a small, plain silk scarf from her bag and started tying knots in the scarf. After tying two to three knots, she asked me whether the scarf looked a bit different than what it did initially.

I said, 'The scarf is the same but its condition is a bit different now.'

'Right,' and she asked, 'Is it possible for me to bring the scarf back to its original form?'

'You will have to untie all the knots first.'

'How should I untie them? Can they be untied by pulling this piece of cloth from both ends?'

'If we find out the points where each knots has been tied exactly, then it will be easier to untie them. But if we pull the scarf from both ends, then we will end up making the knots tighter.'

Purnima gave me a high-five and said, 'Absolutely! We all have fights with our near and dear ones and with many in our social circle. If we insist that only *we* are right, then the knots become stronger and the relationship weaker. If we analyse the reason behind each knot in our relationship and try to address its root cause by talking to the person, then we can easily untie all the knots and our relationship becomes smooth just like this piece of scarf in its original state.'

I was overwhelmed and reached out to hold her hand. She kept her other hand on top of mine and gave me the safe space I needed. When I was composed, I gave her a hug and said, 'I think, I'm going to make a call to a dear friend to untie that knot.'

Knots that you need to untie

Understand the blueprint of the human DNA. To have nurturing relationships in life is a basic human need. Everyone wants to feel valued and acknowledged in a relationship and for any kind of relationship to function optimally, it is important to untie knots the very moment they creep in. Instead of hoping for things to resolve on its own, you must take the first step to untie them.

Miscommunication or rather a lack of communication or the inability to express oneself is often the reason why many relationships go astray.

Think about the close relationships in your life. Do you see any knots? Have you made an effort to untie them?

I am sure you, like many of us, hesitate to take the first step to untie these knots. Eventually, these knots become so tight that it becomes hard to untie them and then we end up losing out on the meaningful bonds in our life.

This reminds me of a heartwarming poem by the renowned poet Muneer Niyazi that captures this thought beautifully. The translation of an excerpt is as follows:

I always delay
The words I should say
The promises I should obey
The one I should call
The one who turned away

I always delay

The shoulder I must offer
The hand I must provide
The long lost ways I must walk
The ones that I had set aside

I always delay...[1]

Are you waiting for someone to step forward to untie those knots? Life is short, you do not know what will happen in the next moment. As clichéd as that sounds. Make an effort to untie the knots and break free from years of pain that you are carrying in your heart. Imagine how beautiful each of your relationship will become if you take that step.

Psychiatrist and Professor of Psychiatry at Harvard Medical School Robert J. Waldinger shared in the Harvard Study of Adult Development that the number one determinant that makes people happier and healthier in life is good relationships. The ongoing Harvard study is considered one of the world's longest studies of adult life, having started in 1938 during the Great Depression. In 2017, he told The Harvard Gazette, 'Taking care of your body is important, *but tending to your relationships is a form of self-care too*. That, I think, is the revelation.'[2]

---

1. Hindi Shiyari, 'Hamesha Der Kar Deta Hoon Main in English', https://www.hindishayari.biz/2020/02/hamesha-der-kar-deta-hoon-main-in-english-hamesha-der-kar-deta-hu-lyrics-in-english.html, accessed on 19 July 2022.
2. Zameena Mejia, 'Harvard's Longest Study Of Adult Life Reveals How You Can Be Happier And More Successful', https://www.cnbc.com/2018/03/20/this-harvard-study-reveals-how-you-can-be-happier-and-more-successful.html#:~:text=Waldinger%2C%20the%20director%20of%20the,1938%20during%20the%20Great%20Depression, accessed on 19 July 2022.

Relationships need to be *taught*

Every relationship has its ups and downs. It is natural to experience those waves, but the real test is how you handle the high tides. In schools, subjects like Maths, Arts, Science are taught but there is no class on relationships. Managing relationships is an essential life skill, but unfortunately it is not taught in schools and colleges.

Happiness Curriculum

Though there is a ray of hope. Some schools are now taking an endeavour to revisit their curriculum and one such commendable effort was taken by the Government of Delhi which launched The Happiness Curriculum in July 2018 with a vision to strengthen the foundations of happiness and well-being for all students through a 35-minute class conducted daily for all students from kindergarten to class 8 across 1,030 government schools in the national capital. The intended outcome is to enhance students' level of awareness, mindfulness and deepen learning to lead a happier and meaningful life and it teaches mindfulness, social–emotional learning and *relationship building*.[3]

---

3. PTI, 'Happiness Curriculum is a 'Massive Success': Sisodia', The Indian Express, 6 September 2021, https://indianexpress.com/article/education/happiness-curriculum-is-a-massive-success-sisodia-7489100, accessed on 4 September 2022.

What is in your cup?

Now imagine that you are holding a cup of black coffee and someone suddenly comes along and bumps into you. You end up spilling the coffee on the floor. The person asks you,

'Why did you spill the coffee?'

You replied, 'Err, because you bumped into me.'

The person smiled and said, 'No, it's a trick question. You spilled black coffee because there was black coffee in your cup. Had there been tea in your cup, you would have spilled tea. Whatever is inside the cup spills out.'

What do you learn from this? Well, the lesson is that people will come in your life to shake you. How you respond to them will be based on what you are carrying inside of you. Most of us live our lives in unconscious reactivity rather than conscious responsiveness.

Ask yourself:

What am I holding in my cup today?

- *Is it peace or anger?*
- *Is it assertive or harsh words?*

Life provides you the cup and *you* choose what you fill it with. When someone is rude to you, you do not have to take it personally because you know that the other person is dishing out what is inside of them, but you do not have to hold a similar cup.

There will be days when you will experience hurt, but how you handle it will depend on how you process your feelings and emotions in that situation.

Dysfunctional ways of dealing with your emotions

Following are the dysfunctional ways of dealing with your feelings during a crisis in a relationship.

Suppressing your feelings

You may suppress your feelings and do not express what you truly feel. You do not speak up when your boundaries are violated by the other person, as if keeping quiet will bring resolution to the problem and the other person will magically discover what you need or feel. If you do not tell people how you feel, how will they know?

Denying your feelings

You go into a denial mode and act as if the problem does not exist at all, making it seem like you are okay with what is happening. When in reality, you know in your heart that you are not content with the behaviour of the other person. Only when you face a problem upfront, can you resolve it. Or at least try to resolve it.

Expressing your feelings with passive aggression

This is the most dangerous way of handling any problem in a relationship. You signal microaggression through eye rolls, raised tone or sarcastic comments, conveying your frustration or anger towards the other person, yet acting as if there is nothing wrong. This makes the situation worse.

Blaming the other person

The easiest way to avoid responsibility for and accountability of a situation is to put the entire blame on the other person. If a person is toxic for you, you must know that you have a choice to walk away instead of blaming them.

Silence

Yes, silence is golden, but when a misunderstanding has popped up in a relationship—silence could be detrimental. Sometimes you may use silence as a weapon to keep the other person guessing or confused about what you really want. Stop using silence as a weapon, express your feelings clearly instead.

It is not me, it is *them*

'They are being the tough ones, not me!'

I often hear my clients tell me this. And they often ask, 'What are the strategies that can make the other person love me or listen to me?'

I hear them patiently and tell them that the first step is self-examination. I can assist you, but I cannot take that step for you. This observation is often met with resistance from them.

'Why do I need to examine *myself* when *they* are the problem?'

When I gently nudge them and ask if they were ever rude to the other person in their relationship, they reply, 'Yes, I was on a few occasions but on those days I was having a bad day.'

Isn't it ironic that we judge others by their behaviour and forgive ourselves by our intention?

I said, 'I agree that the other person might be acting strange. Let us assume 99 per cent of the time it is their fault. But, what about your contribution of 1 per cent to the conflict? Furthermore, what actions do you need to take to make it work? Can you own your share before we handle the other 99 per cent?'

It takes courage and maturity to take responsibility for a rift in a relationship, but therein lies our true healing.

Understand, people cannot read minds, so you need to communicate your needs to them. Also, if the other person in the relationship is so toxic, why are you still holding on to them? It is time to stop asking, *Why are they doing this to me?* and start asking, *Why am I allowing this to happen with me?*

Do not ignore red flags in the beginning because you will eventually leave because of them in the end. Henceforth, call them out the moment you see the first one. 'If you ignore the red flags, embrace the heartache to come.' (Amanda Mosher) How beautifully put.

What is your contribution to your relationships? Are you ready to take ownership of your 1 per cent and take the first step to heal your relationship?

No, I am not dumping all responsibility on you, but the truth is that it is much easier and healthier for you to better yourself because no one else is going to change themselves for you.

How to handle misunderstandings

A better way to handle misunderstandings in a relationship is to ask yourself the following three questions:

What am I feeling? (Emotions)

What do I need? (Needs—Universal)

What is my ask from the other person? (Request)

I call it the FNA Model.

For example, if you are bothered that your dear one does not respond to your messages you could say something along the following lines:

- *I feel* concerned when you do not respond to my message the whole day long
- *I need* to know that you are safe and doing fine
- *Could you please* respond to me by acknowledging my message once?

The most effective way to handle your emotions is to embrace and accept them. Your emotions, like anger, fear, happiness, are physiological response to perceived stimulus whereas your feelings are the physical and mental sensations that arise as a result of responding to those emotions. For example, laughter is a way of experiencing joy, whereas crying is one of the ways to experience sadness. Your emotions come first and feelings come second. And a big part of embracing your feelings is to feel them fully. If you deny or suppress your feelings, they will keep resurfacing and harming you. *You need to feel an emotion fully to heal it completely.* When you understand your own needs better, you will be in a better position to honour others' as well.

'Beneath every behaviour, there is a feeling and beneath each feeling is a need. And when we meet that need rather than focus on the behaviour we begin to deal with the cause, not the symptom.' (Ashleigh Warner)

What makes a relationship great?

Everyone has their own ideas of what a great relationship is about. What seems crazy to someone in a relationship might make complete sense to you. True relationships essentially have the following key elements:

- Love
- Compassion
- Respect
- Trust
- Open communication

If your relationship has these elements, it will be a liberating and empowering bond. A true relationship has the power to heal and bring deeper meaning to your life.

But most importantly, ask yourself what kind of relationship do you share with yourself. Before expecting love from others, first ask yourself these two critical questions:

Do I love myself?

Am I kind to myself?

The capacity with which you love yourself is the capacity with which you show up for others. If you are kind to yourself when you make a mistake, you are more likely to show that kindness and understanding when others make mistakes. Unconditional love does not mean that you should have unconditional acceptance to misbehaviour.

Do you show up as your real self in your connections so that others can show up as who they are, or do you resort to pleasing people by giving small compliments to have them relate to you in a certain way so that they like you and you can fit in?

There is nothing wrong in giving genuine compliments, but flattering people is best avoidable. You will struggle to state your true opinion, or stand up for yourself when it matters the most to you if you are a people pleaser.

Games people play

How others show up in a relationship is up to them, you can let them know, but you cannot change them if they do not want to. You can tell someone what you do not like in their behaviour, but you cannot control it. You can only control your own behaviour.

Ask yourself: *Have I contributed to the toxicity in a relationship by playing an ego game?*

By building awareness around the four common ego games (that you may play knowingly or unknowingly), you can bring a shift in your interactions with others.

Following are the four ego games at play:

I am right

When you are in this mode, you do not like it when someone does not agree to your point of view. The moment someone disagrees with you, you become defensive. You no longer want to listen to what the other person has to say and become rigid in your approach because you believe that you need to have the last word. This approach is harmful for your relationships.

You are wrong

This is the other side of the coin. In this mode, you go out of your way to prove that the other person is wrong. This is detrimental to any bond because people will start to distance themselves from you when you constantly try to prove them wrong instead of finding a middle ground to make things work.

Domination

Dominating others is another ego game that you might play when your needs are not met. In this mode, you make the other person feel guilty by using a tone that is sarcastic and accusing. You may not even be aware of the subtle interference of this ego game in many of your relationships.

Resistance to acceptance

In many instances, you may resist to accept your mistake. And when the other person presents evidence, you avoid any kind of communication and withdraw from the relationship for a while, since you do not want to take ownership.

Whenever you catch yourself falling in the trap of these games, pause and reflect as to how you can act in a more kind and loving manner. If these traps are not avoided, you may end up falling into a downward spiral in your relationships. Become mindful of these ego games and act upon them.

How attached are you?

If I ask you who are you most attached to, who would come to your mind? Now, imagine for a moment that this person does not exist in your life and have decided to move on.

Was it easy letting go of this relationship?

Do you feel anxious about losing this relationship?

Have you been a people pleaser in this relationship because you were afraid of their rejection?

Do you become anxious about doing things without the person around?

If the answer is 'yes' to any of the above questions, you are probably attached to that person. The popular belief suggests that we should not have any kind of attachments, or rather, serious attachments with people, thoughts or things. Attachment is the emotional dependence we have on people or material things with a certain degree of our survival interwoven into the thing or person we hold so dear. And not all attachments are bad for you. It is all about how you handle them that can be either harmful or fulfilling for you.

Many new age self-help books and the social media feed the idea that we *should* and *must* be entirely emotionally self-sufficient. Of course, it is vital not to rely on others for validation or approval, but you must understand that humans are social beings. And having a sense of belonging and nourishing connections is what makes us human and helps us thrive. You cannot spend your life in isolation with only your own thoughts for company. After all, it took two people to bring one person in this world.

Real enlightment happens through our relationships (with others and with ourselves).

What is your attachment style?

What is a healthy or unhealthy attachment?

If you view attachment as a strong connection with someone that helps you to function to your optimum capacity without total dependence on them, that is simply amazing! We are driven to find emotional security with other people just like we are driven to gather food for our survival. Emotional security is intrinsic to our survival too. Any relationship between adults becomes problematic when there is one-sided dependence, either economic or psychological.

The sweet spot is where you strike the right balance between giving and taking in a relationship.

Sweet Spot

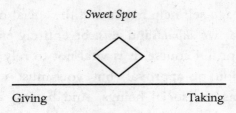

Giving   Taking

What is in your fist?

In my early twenties, I was not someone who would worry about my attachment style or its impact on me. But my outlook changed when I had to let go of someone who was constantly draining me. I found myself stuck between not wanting to hurt them and putting myself first. In one way or another, this stress affected different areas of my life.

It was a typical day at work and I was attending a team meeting. I was a bit lost and my boss sensed that I was not paying attention fully. He asked me to stay back to work on a project; and to my surprise, asked me, 'Is everything okay with you, Nancy?

I replied, 'Yes, Sir.'

But he did not seem convinced. He was, after all, wise and perceptive.

He said, 'Maybe, you are being honest. And maybe not.'

He then smiled.

'Nancy, let me tell you a story about the monkey and the jar. Don't chuckle, okay?'

I nodded.

He said, 'There was a monkey who saw a jar filled with groundnuts. The jar had a narrow opening and was attached to a table. The monkey grabbed the groundnuts. I mean, what a way to maximise on an opportunity, right? He then saw a man approaching him with a stern look, so he tried to quickly take his fist out of the jar as hard as he could, but failed. Ultimately, he was caught and taken to a zoo. If only the monkey would let go of the groundnuts and open his fist, he would have easily escaped. *What are you attached to that you are finding hard to let go?*'

The question jolted me to the core. I reflected on it. *How do I let go of a friendship of several years. How do I tackle being alone? What will my peers say?*

At that time, I simply did not have faith in my ability to nurture better friendships and start afresh.

I am sure many of you live with this idea: regretting about letting go of a relationship that could have worked. That is a waste of your time. If it could have worked, it *should* have worked and it *would* have worked. If it was meant to happen, *it would have happened.*

I thanked him for helping me realise that it is important to let go of the 'groundnut' in my jar for greater personal happiness and freedom. Ever since, I have not looked back at that toxic relationship. Letting go of it was the best decision of my life.

There are many lessons to be learned when you hand over power to someone else. And I learnt mine. *Why was I not choosing myself before others?*

Know that you will outgrow some friends. That is how life works, so do not feel guilty about it. You may have to lose a few people in your life to find yourself.

Ask yourself:

Am I holding on to anything in my jar?

What do I need to let go of in my life?

'Toxic relationships are like a good pasta that has been overcooked,' said the bestselling author Dr Asa Don Brown.

How true! Be hungry for good, healthy relationships.

Because you will suffer if you become too dependent on certain people. You must value and love your near and dear ones; however, the problem begins the moment you attach your identity to them. This is not a fruitful way to look at relationships. The better way to understand your relationships is by understanding your own attachment style.

Attachment is not just with people. It could be with clothes despite being fully aware that they do not fit you and will not fit you in the future. This is what is called sunk-cost fallacy—discussed in an earlier chapter. We tend to do this because we *think* it provides us with some sense of security by being with things, people, thoughts that are familiar, and letting go of what is familiar seems like a big task.

If you think that you must stay in a toxic relationship after spending years on it just because it will serve you some day, then you need to wake up! Only when you take a step to move out of your comfort zone and step into uncharted territories, will you be truly liberated.

Now I know some of you may be financially dependent on someone and moving away may not seem like the right decision at a particular point and that is understandable. What you can do instead is to take small steps every day to make yourself financially independent and then take a call.

Your attachment pattern

Your life is a function of how you show up in your relationships. Your personal life, your career, your health, your finances, it is all about the kind of relationship you share with *yourself*.

Did any kind of attachment to people in my life cause me pain?

Hell yes! Though, on self-reflection and through my healing journey, I realised that majority of the times I was the one who was tolerating nonsense in the relationship: be it at work, in friendships or in other personal relationships. I was finding it hard to let go because of the fear of being alone. Author and songwriter Charlotte Eriksson expressed this so beautifully: 'Don't light yourself on fire trying to brighten someone else's existence.' Most of my relationships were just a mirror reflection of the kind of relationship I shared with myself. I was being hard on myself and voila, I attracted similar kinds of friendships, bosses and clients in my life.

Do you find similar patterns operating in your life?

Use the hurt you experienced to change how you show up in your connections with others for better.

Stop lying to yourself

How we feel in a relationship is often a result of an underlying need that we fail to express ourselves. Healthy relationships require uncomfortable conversations *too*.

Fyodor Dostoevsky famously said, 'Lying to ourselves is more deeply ingrained than lying to others.'

How true.

By choosing to be in emotionally draining relationships, you are adding to misery in your life. Why? It is your choice, if the relationship is suffocating and you do not like it, change it. Do not feel sad about outgrowing people who had the chance to grow with you.

Relationships require *nurture* just like *nature*. If you do not water your plants, they die; the same logic is applicable for your relationships.

Fake bonds on social media

I read somewhere on Twitter the other day: 'Relationships are harder now because conversations become texting, arguments become phone calls, and feelings become status updates.'

Relationship inventory exercise

Create an inventory of your relationships and see what actions need to be taken on them:

List individuals that nourish you and the ones that drain you. Now, next to the individuals that drain you, mention why you are still holding on to these connections and what could be some of the reasons that make it hard for you to let go of such draining connections.

Nourishing Relationships	Draining Relationships
Name	Name ....
Name	Name ....

Let go of people who do not allow you to lead your life fully and are toxic.

Don't we all need help?

Sometimes, we all need support and help in our relationships though we hesitate to ask for them. One of my friends is very comfortable asking for help. While writing this chapter, I called her up to ask her how asking for help comes so naturally to her. She narrated a wonderful story:

Once a couple was returning from a mall after buying some groceries. On the way they saw a scruffily-dressed lady sitting in a corner, who appeared to be poor and sad. As they crossed her, they were certain that the lady would ask them for some money, but she did not. So, the couple reversed the car and asked the lady if she needed any help.

The lady said, 'Don't we all?'

After she narrated this story, it became easy for me to ask for help.

'You complete me...?'

Hell, NO!

Yes, it does sound romantic when Tom Cruise utters these words in the movie *Jerry Maguire*. But while caring for and showing affection for someone is wonderful, attaching your identity to them can be damaging for you. As social beings, we thrive on social connections, but these connections should not be ones that consume us and make us entirely dependent on the other person. You can hold a million connections and yet remain independent or interdependent in your relationships.

Avoid excessive emotional reliance on your close ones at the cost of your personal needs. Do not seek validation from anyone, as if your survival depends on their constant approval. Dependents usually operate from low self-esteem and constantly feel that there is something lacking in their lives, so they seek happiness by constantly seeking approval from their loved one(s).

On the other hand, interdependence is where two individuals care for each other and nurture the relationship without sacrificing their personal needs. People who are interdependent understand that no one 'completes' them, their near and dear ones are just an added bonus in their journey of life.

And finally, independence refers to the empowering self-belief that you can handle difficult situations and are free from external control, not subjecting yourself to dominance by anyone.

The key is to find synergy between interdependence and independence.

Relationship Scale

Dependent.................Interdependent............Independent

Do not look outside yourself to fill your cup or feel complete. No one can really make you happy, they can only support you in your happiness. Interdependence is a healthy way of building relationships wherein each person has the space to be themselves, the liberty to make their choices.

There is this famous scene from the movie *The Perks of Being a Wallflower* where Charlie asks his English teacher Bill Anderson, 'Mr Anderson, why do nice people choose the wrong people to date?'

Mr Anderson replies, 'Well, we accept the love we think we deserve.'

Not letting go of a toxic relationship can often be a survival strategy. However, you must keep reminding yourself that you deserve to offer the love to yourself that you offer to others.

At the same time, take responsibility if you have contributed towards a misunderstanding. Do not be a victim and take control of your reality. No knight (or angel) is coming to save you from yourself, you have to be your own angel.

To the people who believe that 'time heals everything', I would beg to differ and say it is you who heals yourself, and true healing occurs when you befriend yourself and accept and embrace all parts of yourself as valid.

Remember, when you say 'I love you' to someone, the word 'I' comes before the word 'you'. It is time to let go of what does not serve you any more and get back to yourself and be free.

What do you need to stop tolerating in your relationships and what is your 1 per cent that you need to take responsibility for?

....

....

....

....

....

....

....

....

....

....

6

HOW TO CREATE AN INNER SHIFT

The Journey Explained

'Success is not final, failure is not fatal: it is the courage to continue that counts.'

—Winston S. Churchill

You have reached this far with me. Great! Welcome to the ultimate chapter on inner shift.

How do you address an aspect in your life that needs to be changed?

Ignore it?

or

Acknowledge it and do something about it?

What is the right option? Well, if you want to improve yourself, you will choose the second option. Remember, *you* are solely responsible for your own development—no one, but *you*.

Be action-oriented

'The path to success is to take massive, determined action,' said Tony Robbins, top life and business strategist and *New York Times* bestselling author. You must have saved screenshots or made notes on meaningful quotes about life, promising yourself to look at them later and take action on them sooner.

Did you?

No?

You know why?

Here is why: Just saving profound quotes does not bring any change. Acting upon them does. You can usher in change in your life with awareness, acceptance and, most importantly, with some *action*. If you want to create that much needed inner shift, you must take some actions. *Pronto!*

Adopt the momentum principle of success

An inner shift is no instant noodles. It takes time to develop it. It is the result of behaviours and actions implemented over a period of time on a consistent basis. When you start to practise a new behaviour and follow it daily, you trigger the momentum principle of success. 'Although it may take tremendous amounts of energy to overcome inertia and get going initially, it then takes far less energy to keep going.'[1]

If you do not have a clear objective or framework you fail to create a sustainable change in your behaviour. At one point of time, I used to be great at commencing things but never

1. Archive for the Momentum Principle of Success Category, 'Behind the Scenes/Virtual COO', Robert Finkelstein, 10 August 2010, https://robertfinkelstein.wordpress.com/category/momentum-principle-of-success/, 10 August 2010, accessed on 5 August 2022.

finishing them until one of my clients held up the mirror and said, 'Why should I follow any of your advice if I don't see you doing it yourself?'

That almost felt like a smack on my face!

I am sure you, like many of us, like to offer unsolicited advice on how others can improve their lives. But do you follow your own advice that you generously proffer others? The first step towards embracing a new behaviour is to take charge of yourself one day at a time. If you make healthy choices every day, healthy habits would stay eventually.

Questions that you need to ask yourself

Ask yourself the following questions. (I have answered a couple of these else you will not start.)

What change do I want to bring in my life?

Who is going to bring this change?   This is obvious, *you*

Why do I want to bring this change?   ....

....

....

When do I want to bring this change?   From *today* itself

A critical question seems to be missing here. *How* do I usher in the required change? The following section will help answer this question.

Framework for change

Before we get to how to create the desired change, ask yourself: *How badly do I want to change?*

I cannot tell you how many of my first calls with clients begin with them telling me, 'I am aware of my problem area, but I just need some sort of process or guide to deal with it.' This makes complete sense because we all need to find a framework to support our lifestyles in a more meaningful way.

After training people from all walks of life for close to two decades, I have observed that the transformational journey of my clients had been a step-by-step process that helped them achieve the life they desired. After studying all case studies, I saw a framework emerge, which I call the A5 framework. This addresses the HOW part of forming a new behaviour and creating the much desired inner shift.

This effective and doable and inclusive framework comprises the following 5 A's:

1. Awareness of self
2. Acceptance
3. Anchor
4. Action
5. Accountability

Awareness + Acceptance + Anchor + Action + Accountability
= Inner Shift

When applied in this sequence, the framework helps you to change an undesirable pattern in your life that you have been meaning to change. The first two steps are important for inner discovery and the remaining ones are where the actual execution happens.

One step leads to another and the inner shift is unachievable if even one step is missing. The steps are explained in detail in the subsequent sections.

Step 1: Awareness of Self

Have you ever been able to see your reflection in moving water? It is only when the water is still and clear, can you see your reflection in it. Similarly, research suggests that only when you see yourself clearly, you become more confident to take new actions. Clarity for oneself comes with self-awareness. Self-awareness is the conscious knowledge of oneself.

Leading our lives with full awareness

Once the CEO of a successful start-up, told me, 'Nancy, most of us are warmly settled into our comfort zones and blame our mundanity or mistakes on the system, society for not realising our full potential.' He added, 'We can utilise the same energy that we use to complain and redirect it to take a step forward towards becoming who we want to be.'

Four reservoirs of energy

Another effective way to enhance your self-awareness is by consciously focusing on your energy. There are four areas of your life from where you gain energy. These also drain your energy. So, how do you find time to do what you love when you are so exhausted at the end of the day? The short answer is you will find time and energy for what is most important to you if you have enough energy to do it.

When you say you do not have enough time, often you are hinting that you do not have enough energy to take an action or it is not your priority.

No framework will work long term if your energy reserves are depleted. Every day you wake up with a certain amount of physical, mental, emotional and social energy. And they are your reservoirs of energy. They can be described as follows:

1. *Physical:* the quantity of energy

2. *Emotional:* the quality of energy

3. *Mental:* the focus of energy

4. *Social*: the force of energy

For instance, if you do not get enough sleep, do not exercise or do not eat healthy, your physical energy will be depleted. Similarly, how you feel about yourself and the feelings you get from the tasks you are engaged in can enhance or deplete your emotional energy. If you do things that bring you inner peace, you will naturally feel good. How you manage your emotions will have an impact on your relationships and thus every aspect of your life. To have better focus on the task at hand, you need to channelise your thoughts; in other words, work on your mental models and reflect on the kind of social relationships you want to nurture in life. Building and nurturing social relationships are critical because some people will bring out the best in you whereas others will encourage you to follow habits that are detrimental to you.

'Look outside and you will see yourself. Look inside and you will find yourself.' (Drew Gerald)

How Self-aware Are You?

Before you bring in change in your life, you need to be self-aware. Deep down, you probably have a pretty good sense of what you would like to change in yourself. I am sure you must have considered it quite often, not in a fixated, obsessed kind of way, but as a droopy resignation that crosses your mind during the quiet moments when you are alone.

How do you find a solution to your problem?

Simple.

Become aware of the real underlying issue. So, the first step in bringing in any change in your behaviour is being self-aware. Being conscious of your identity, your thoughts, your habits and your self-image is part of being self-aware.

Being mindful and raising your self-awareness is the ability to stay in the present and not identifying yourself with memories and worries of the future. The more aware you are about your internal world, the more conscious you will become of the impact your internal world has on your external world. Most of us live with the idea that we have a great understanding of who we are, though a study by Harvard found that even though most people believe they are self-aware, only 10–15 per cent of the people they studied during their research actually fit the criteria. Isn't that surprising?

Overthinking

I am sure now your inner voice is arguing: *But I introspect and reflect regularly*.

I am sure you do. But are you doing it the right way?

Are you self-reflecting or overthinking?

Many think that they are self-reflecting but actually they are overthinking. To quote Fyodor Dostoyevsky, 'To think too much is a disease.'

Overthinking does not solve any problem; in fact, it aggravates it and that could be the reason you keep seeing the same results while expecting something totally different.

How to bring in more self-awareness?

Sit down.

Make a note of your daily activities that you do without being conscious about them; in others words, in autopilot mode. For instance, the first thing some of us do when we wake up is check our phone or drink tea. Once you become aware of such habits, you will realise what needs to shift. If you do not want to check your phone first thing in the morning, then place it just outside your bedroom. Now you must be thinking *what about the alarm*? Well, since your phone is right outside your bedroom, you will have to get up to turn it off in the morning and voila, you are up and awake!

Once you understand the pattern of the behaviours in auto-pilot mode, you can analyse which habits need to be replaced with more conscious choices. Now, do not fall into the trap of blaming yourself, become conscious of what is not serving you and take charge of your life instead. Ask yourself: *What can I do **right now**.*

Change the narrative. Stop asking yourself: *Why do I follow unhealthy habits?*

Instead ask: *What new behaviours should I inculcate?*

Write down two behaviours that you want to inculcate in your life.

Yes, *only* two.

Narrowing down on two may seen tough but implementing the change might be tougher if we list down 10–12 behaviours instead of just two.

20-second exercise

Struggling? If not, you may skip this section. If yes, then follow the 20-second exercise. You have twenty seconds to make a note of behaviours that you are currently struggling with. After twenty seconds are over, look at the list and narrow it down to only two behaviours. The beauty of this exercise is that you do not overthink the question, and you note down whatever comes naturally to you, and this is more often than not your current reality.

Your twenty seconds start now!

After you are done, think of specific actions to combat the behaviours. Be realistic and opt for behaviours that can help you to lead a more fulfilling life.

Once you become more aware of the two behaviours that you would like to inculcate in your life, you move on to the next step: Acceptance.

Step 2: Acceptance

It takes a long while to accept yourself fully.

You do not accept that you are perfectly capable of bringing in the required change.

You do not accept that you have the light within you, waiting to shine.

You do not accept that change is really not that hard as you make it to be.

Inculcating a new behaviour may not appear easy, but it is not that difficult either. Between the easy and the difficult is a zone that I call the Doable Zone. If something is doable, then you will gather the resources needed, you change the game. Do not call something hard or difficult—say it is doable.

Do not just acknowledge your habits detrimental to yourself.

Are you committed to changing them or are you just eager?

One of the main reasons you remain stuck in habits you know do not serve you any more is because of the thoughts that lull you into a comfort zone, such as, 'One ice cream a day won't kill me', or 'I only drink like a crazy person on weekends', or 'Let me binge-watch one more season'. These thoughts convince you that there is nothing wrong with your behaviour, even though you know it is not serving you well. You use your bad habits to avoid dealing with something more meaningful.

There is no such thing as half-acceptance, you have to fully accept how some habits are not for your greater good only then will you start working on developing new thoughts and behaviours.

Do you struggle to accept a difficult situation or a shortcoming in yourself?

You may be aware that you need to change but are in denial. *You are not alone.*

Accepting difficult things about yourself or your life could be scary at times and staying in your current reality may appear to be an easier path. Being kind to yourself and having faith that you can do it, is the key.

Once you accept that there is one key area that needs a shift, you will start the process of decluttering. 'The first step in crafting the life you want is to get rid of everything you don't.' (Joshua Becker)

Have you noticed how sometimes your laptop starts to run slow because of the truckload of files on its hard drive? And when you take it for repair, the technician tells you to delete unwanted files for better performance of your laptop. You must have said, 'I've done that already, but it's simply not helping.' He then suggests that your laptop may require complete formatting by deleting all files and uploading a new software. You go ahead with it and after the formatting, you have much more space for new files and the performance of your laptop is enhanced.

Have you ever done that with your thoughts, habits and relationships with yourself and others?

Try it.

Sit down and declutter your life.

If you continue to do things that are not serving you well, then your energy will get depleted and you will fail to unlock your potential.

Let go of those energy-depleting 'files' on your system, then you will find your anchor.

Step 3: Anchor

Anchor is a signal that triggers or alerts your brain to initiate an action or follow a certain behaviour.

Anchors could be visual cues, empowering thoughts, sounds or signals in your external environment. Let us say you feel like snacking. And you cannot wait to unpack that packet of salted, cream potato chips. But if you have stock of dry fruits at your home, you will have them instead. This is an example of your environment acting as a trigger for you to act in a certain manner.

Your thoughts act as anchors too.

Picture this: You have a presentation to give. There are two ways of approaching this. You could be anxious about failing or you could prepare thoroughly for the presentation, eager to share your ideas. If you are worried about failure, you might procrastinate whereas thorough preparation will take you on the path to progress.

These anchor thoughts guide and drive your efforts and actions. Anchor thoughts are your driving force.

A big ship is stopped from drifting into the sea by an anchor. Similarly, an anchor is meant to hold you steady and keep you away from wandering into unapproved behaviours.

Anchor and emotional state

Anchors help you go into a certain state of being. Athletes use anchor thoughts to get back into regular practice zones to regain peak performances in a game. Former captain of the Indian national cricket team Virat Kohli mentioned in one of his interviews as to how he uses visualisation as a technique during his practice sessions to get into a desired state on the playing field.[2] Relying on visual sensory data is the most common form of anchoring.

Positive anchors evoke pleasant feelings and motivate you to change your mental state. Anchors are built by repetition and association. For instance, imagine yourself driving a car and you reach the signal and the traffic light turns red. What do you do? You have learned to stop and wait in front of the traffic light until it turns green. Through your experience of following the rules you have learnt that when you see a red traffic light, you stop. And the moment it turns green, you proceed your way. In other words, you are conditioned in this specific event.

Similarly, you can choose unique spaces as anchors that can move you to a particular kind of action. For example, when I decided to work on my book, I asked myself which area of my house could help me to write on a consistent basis and help me maintain my focus. After narrowing down on a specific

2. Visualization - the secret, 'Visualization used by Virat Kohli', https://www.youtube.com/watch?v=X-XAvCkQ4Zo, YouTube video, 1:30, 26 November 2020.

corner of my house, I created a dedicated writing desk with inspirational quotes, a white board with my To-do Tasks. So my space acted as an anchor and every time I sat on the chair next to the desk at specific timings, I was motivated to write. I repeated the anchoring exercise 5–6 times to strengthen the anchor. So specific timing associated with this dedicated place followed by an action of writing helped me anchor to a mental state of writing with focus.

Whenever you act on a stimulus or urge, you are strengthening the wiring of that behaviour in your mind. An anchor creates an emotional stimulus for your body, which helps you to feel elated and take action. To strengthen your anchor, you should practise it multiple times. The more you repeat a specific anchoring process, the more it will improve your performance and lead to an automatic response.

Emotion is energy in motion. Every emotion you feel has a certain physiology associated with it. Have you noticed your posture, breathing and facial expressions when you are happy? Emotional anchors can be created at any moment, even right now.

The brain is wired to prefer joy over pain. And sometimes indulging in unhealthy habits, like munching on your favourite chips, gives you immense joy. However, if you want to change this habit, you need to associate a positive anchor alert with it. It could be 'If I eat healthy, I'll stay fit and energetic. Visualise the joy you are experiencing when you follow healthy eating on a daily basis.' Such anchor alerts can bring some meaningful change in your life.

If you rehearse with tremendous positive emotional intensity, you will carve out a new neural pathway in your brain to form a new habit. Your brain will produce new results only if you practise positive anchoring on a consistent basis. If you do not do this, you will relapse into the old, self-destructive pattern of behaviour.

Several studies suggest that your brain cannot tell the difference between something you imagine and something you experience, hence anchoring a behavioural change linked to a positive emotion can be transformational.

Dr Lawrence Katz at Duke University lab, Durham, North Carolina observed in a research that the simplest way to create improved neural pathways in the brain was to do neurobics exercises that create new connections in our brains.[3]

In a neurobics exercise, you practise a new activity that you want to inculcate (let us say, drinking warm water instead of coffee) and pair it with an emotion you would like to feel (like celebration). Neurobics exercises snap your brain into attention by breaking old patterns. This will become clear with the popular model called Pavlov Classical Conditioning.

---

3. Anonymous.,'Neurobics, The Unique New Science Of Brain Exercises', Keep Your Brain Alive, http://www.keepyourbrainalive.com/, accessed on 30 August 2022.

Pavlov Classical Conditioning model

Pavlov Classical Conditioning model was an experiment conducted by Russian physiologist Ivan Pavlov. He won the 1904 Nobel Prize in Physiology. While conducting his experiment, Pavlov observed that every time he entered a room with dogs, the canines would salivate as they associated Pavlov's presence in the room with food being served. He then introduced the sound of the bell whenever he fed his dogs and after several repetitions, the dogs would salivate as soon as they heard the sound of the bell, even when the food was not served to them.

This is an excellent example to understand how anchor-alert (stimulus) creates a response when we are exposed to that anchor repeatedly. Anchor is a prompt that inspires you to take action. Any task that does not charge you up will not make you feel energised enough to take any action. You may have noticed how at times no matter how powerful your urges are, wisdom has guided you to not act on them, and you ended up making a different and a better choice.

Think of two anchor thoughts that you can create corresponding to the habit that you want to change. Once you have identified your anchors, it is important to act upon them on a consistent basis. And this brings us to Step 4.

Step 4: Action

What is that small action that you can take to achieve your goal? If you want progress in your life, you have to take action. You just cannot store all powerful ideas in your mind—you need to apply them as well. *Awareness, acceptance, anchor thoughts minus action is of no use.*

Progress Principle

Teresa M. Amabile and Steven J. Kramer of Harvard Business School did a rigorous analysis of nearly 12,000 diary entries provided by 238 employees in seven companies[4] and they came up with *The Progress Principle,* a book based on their study. It suggests that small, forward momentum creates the best lives. Small and steady wins create progress and make people happy, motivated and productive.

Actions and anchors go hand in hand. Your actions should be about taking small, daily steps towards unlocking your awesomeness. This will help break stagnation in your life. Do not be distracted or procrastinate. Even the word 'distraction' ends with action. I am sure that you want to take action to inculcate a new habit, but you are trapped by what I call the 3Ps. They are:

Procrastination: When you sit for hours and hours together ruminating about a task and postpone taking any action. Ask yourself these two questions:

---

4. Havard Business Review, 'Store', https://store.hbr.org/product/the-progress-principle-using-small-wins-to-ignite-joy-engagement-and-creativity-at-work/10106, accessed on 31 August.

What is the one thing I can do right now?

And what will be the consequence if I do not do this?

<u>Protection</u> of oneself or self-preservation: Sometimes you tend to protect yourself by delaying a task to avoid the discomfort associated with it. This could just be a made-up story that you have formed in your mind without even trying to experience the situation because of your underlying fears. As a popular quote goes, 'You are not afraid of new love, you're afraid of the old pain.' Ask yourself: *What action can I take that will make me feel more safe while doing this task?*

<u>Perfection</u>: Instead of striving for perfection, strive for excellence. But sometimes by setting high standards, you end up delaying doing anything at all because your mind has set a fixed idea of doing things in a particular way. Procrastination is the best friend of 'perfection'. I am sure you must have heard people say many times: 'Either I will do this perfectly or not do it at all.' And then seen them not take any action at all and the real reason is not seeking perfection, <u>it is fear of failure</u>. Remember, a small step at a time is better than a giant step in a given moment. Ask yourself: *<u>What can I do to produce quality work rather than perfect work?</u>*

To break this cycle of 3Ps, you need another P called Progress. Progress is about taking action to move forward. When you begin to see daily progress, you will develop faith in the process and then you will notice how naturally a new behaviour fits into your life.

Once you have started the process of forming healthy habits, you would need the last and the most important A (accountability) in the framework to ensure that you continue to stay on the path of progress.

Step 5: Accountability

Accountability is being responsible for what you do. It is about holding an intention for your behaviours on a consistent basis. The clearer you are about your intention, the more likely you are to stay consistent.

You can make yourself accountable by ensuring that you realise that at all times you are responsible for your actions. If you are struggling with that, then ask yourself:

What stops me from being accountable?

How do I become more accountable?

Who can help me to become accountable?

I am reminded of the lines from the movie *The Matrix,* when Morpheus says to Neo, 'There's a difference between knowing the path and walking the path.'

I remember it was the end of November 2013, when I was curating a talk for a popular singer from Bollywood, and I asked her how she was able to sustain in the industry for so long. She said, 'I don't take my success for granted, I practise my music every single day.' She further added that many people do not achieve what they want to simply because they are afraid of responsibilities, but she was not. You are either full in or full out, there is no in-between.

Now ask yourself: *Am I full in?*

If you follow the A5 framework, you will be able to break patterns that deplete your energy. This framework will help you create personal power and help you lead a fulfilled life.

As you begin to practise this framework, it is very likely that on some occasions you might be tempted to fall back to your old habits. Relax! Remember to be gentle with yourself in those weak moments. Let self-love be the starting point when you are trying to inculcate any change. It is a natural tendency to subjugate ourselves to judgement if the desired goal is not reached. When you find yourself doing that, take a pause and bring your thoughts back to your intent and ask yourself: *Why did you start the journey of cultivating a new habit in the first place?*

This will surely motivate you to break the cycle of negative self-talk and take the right action.

Let me share an empowering scene from the book, *Boy, the Mole, the Fox, and the Horse*. A boy and a horse were in the woods when the boy said to the horse, 'I can't see a way through.'

Horse asked, 'Can you see your next step?'

'Yes,' said the boy.

'Just take that first step,' said the boy.

What is your next step?

....

....

....

....

....

....

....

....

....

....

7

TO A MORE COURAGEOUS AND AN AUTHENTIC YOU

Right Here, Right NOW

'It takes courage to grow up and become who you really are.'

— E.E. Cummings

How to achieve the impossible

'You will not be able to do it. It's impossible'[1] — these were the words Nimsdai Purja, a Nepal-born naturalised British mountaineer and the holder of multiple mountaineering world records, heard when he shared his goal with colleagues and mountaineering experts. His goal was to complete the climb of fourteen peaks above 8,000m in six months. Jerzy Kukuczka holds the world record to climb them consecutively in seven years, eleven months and fourteen days in 1987. Nims refused to give up. He would not know until he tried. So, in 2019, Nims went ahead with his team and in six months, six days he completed the mission he had set for himself by exceeding the previous goal by a huge margin. How? Why? Because 'a quitter never wins and a winner never quits' as Napeleon Hill the bestselling author of *Think and Grow Rich* rightly observed. Nims motivation to take up this lofty goal was to show to the world that nothing is impossible. He wanted Nepalese climbers to get greater recognition and challenge his own limits.

'The purpose to do this mission was to break boundaries, discover what I am capable of doing and there was a healthy fear that gave me strength to strive and kept me

1. Personal Projects, 'Bremont Project Possible', NIMSDAI, https://www.nimsdai.com/bremont-project-possible, accessed on 1 Septemebr 2022.

alive through the course of this mission,' said Nims in one of his interviews after conquering fourteen of the highest peaks in mere six odd months through sheer hard work, his team's support, his physical and mental fitness, training and determination.

In 2012, Nimsdai Purja climbed a mountain for the first time. Seven years later, he changed the face of mountaineering by scaling all fourteen peaks above 8,000m in just six months and he was just getting started. On 16 January 2021, Nims and his team became the first in history to summit the world's second highest mountain, K2, in winter.[2]

There are many examples of people like Nims from all walks of life who brave out, beating all odds to reach a goal that was considered nearly impossible to begin with. So what is it with people like Nims who pursue such lofty goals with courage and take action in spite of the associated fear?

There are three common strategies people like Nims follow:

One of the *most important* strategies they follow is to stay in the present, focus on the task that is in front of them and take action in the present instead of worrying about what happened in the past or what will happen in the future.

2. Tom Guise and Matt Ray, 'Behind Nirmal Purja's Record-breaking Mountaineering Challenge', Redbull.com, 15 February 2021, https://www.redbull.com/in-en/theredbulletin/nirmal-purja-project-possible-mountaineering-challenge-interview, accessed on 9 August 2022.

The *second* strategy is how they speak to themselves when they face a challenge, that is called self-talk. It is how you speak to yourself when you are faced with a challenge or an opportunity. Let us say you have to give a public lecture. And this is making you anxious, since you find this to be challenging. How do you want to deal with the challenge? You could simply throw your hands up in the air and declare that you cannot do public speaking, or you could start speaking to smaller groups of people. You may face a similar issue with networking. You find it to be challenging as well. You could simply resign to the fact that you are bad at networking, or you could start connecting with like-minded people. There are always two different ways of looking at a situation. The way you perceive something has a strange way of flipping the situation entirely.

And *final* strategy is their ability to take a leap of faith and seek opportunities and strive for goals outside their comfort zone, not worrying about the final outcome. They keep moving towards their goal by putting in their best efforts daily.

I know, I know. There could be situations where despite your sincere attempts of seeking new opportunities, there will be times when you will miss an opportunity. But missing an opportunity once does not mean it is the end of the world. Richard Branson puts it so aptly, 'Opportunities are like buses; there's always another coming around.'

Your perception will always precede action. Feeling uncomfortable, leaving behind what is comfortable can feel strange at first, but stepping out of your comfort zone is an invitation to strive for something greater and tap into your highest potential.

You are not born full of immense courage, no one is, it is the muscle you build one day at a time. I am sure you will agree that to become better at something takes consistent effort and practice. Facing your fears and building courage are no different.

Do not look back in fear

It was around six in the morning when I heard my phone ringing. It was my client Anaya (name changed for privacy). As I answered the call, and without saying hello, she immediately asked if she could have an urgent appointment with me. I quickly checked my calendar and immediately booked a coaching session with her for nine that morning.

Three hours later, Anaya walked in and said, 'You asked me in our last session if there is an incident that has been acting as a roadblock in my path. I know exactly what it is now!'

She sounded excited and I waited with bated breath.

I said, 'Tell me.'

She said, 'I vividly remember this incident, when I was in ninth grade. My English teacher encouraged me to participate in a public speaking contest and I jumped at the opportunity. The D-day arrived and I eagerly went on the stage. But froze. For the first few seconds, I spoke nothing. My mind went completely blank. I still remember the judges and students staring at me, imploring me with their looks to speak something at least. After 7–8 seconds had passed, I don't know what got into me but I started the speech and finished it somehow.

'My teacher was waiting for me in the staff-room. She was visibly furious. She strode up to me and blamed herself for wasting such a great opportunity on me. She regretted not giving the opportunity to a more deserving student.

'I could only manage an apology and walked away without waiting for her to complete. Is forgetting a sign of weakness? Did I do anything wrong?'

I looked at her and I moved my head sideways, signalling No.

Anaya seemed relieved.

She said, 'Exactly! I was just a kid. And it was my first time speaking in front of so many people. That incident ingrained in me a belief that I have to be perfect to start something, else I will end up paying a heavy price. This message till date is deeply imprinted in my mind.'

She paused. And wiped away a big, fat tear trickling down her cheek.

She then took a deep breath and said, 'You know for many years, I carried an underlying fear of getting hurt and being rejected. As a result, I don't speak up in meetings even if I know what to say. I am terrified that if I speak, others will think negatively about me, they won't accept me and I'll be left all alone. Lack of courage in me comes from the fear of rejection and failure.'

There was a pregnant pause in the room.

She threw her hands up in the air and asked, 'Tell me what else I could have done after facing such humiliation as a child? Doesn't such an incidence scar one for life?'

I said, 'I hear you. How can you show up differently now?'

Anaya seemed taken aback. She looked up at the ceiling and said, 'I have been meaning to start from some place and take the first step to face my fear. But how do I even begin?

I said, 'Anaya, relax. Now imagine if your best friend was facing a similar situation, what advice would you give her?'

She thought for a second, smiled and said, 'Well, I will tell my friend to initiate conversations and share her ideas in personal settings to rebuild her confidence...but before she does that she needs to acknowledge her fear, be aware that it is coming from something that happened in the past because without that awareness the fear only grows bigger.'

I smiled and nodded in approval.

I said, 'Remember, that incident happened in the past. You are no longer in the past; you are in the present moment. That incident did happen, yes it did but *in the past*. And the past is gone.'

Moreover, fear and hope cannot function together.

She left the session that day a lot relieved and calmer. In the evening, I received a text message from her saying, 'Nancy, thank you, we always have a choice and next time I will ensure that I move out of my comfort zone and not be fearful, the past is gone and I can make the present way, way better.'

What is your fear story?

Has any past incident scarred you for life?

Are you still holding on to that traumatic incident from your past?

Does that stop you from taking the first step in the right direction?

What do you fear?

....

....

....

....

....

26/11: a survivor's tale

The mere mention of the numbers 26/11 fills our mind with horror and fear. And our hearts swell with immense gratitude and respect for the staff of Taj Mahal Palace Hotel, Mumbai, who displayed great courage during the attack. One such person was Mallika Jagad, a twenty-four-year-old woman who saved sixty lives during the attack at Taj. She was assistant banquet manager at the Taj Hotel at the time. In one of her interviews she shared, 'Before the 26/11 experience, I had no idea that I can be so calm and think clearly even in the face of imminent danger. As I now tell everyone, I realised that night, that we should never give up hope, until the very end.'[3]

The Taj Hotel staff re-defined customer service that day.

Hope is the super mantra.

How to fear less

In my many interactions with people, be that with C-suite executives, corporate professionals, celebrities, homemakers or parents of teenagers, one topic that almost always comes up is how to build the muscle of courage and become fearless.

---

3. Sayantani Nath, 'On 26/11, This 24-Yr-Old Woman Single-Handedly Saved More Than 60 Lives', TheBetterIndia.com, 17 September 2019, https://www.thebetterindia.com/195443/26-11-mumbai-attacks-taj-hotel-unsung-hero-woman-saved-sixty-lives-india/, accessed on 8 August 2022.

And when I ask them what is stopping them from overcoming their fear? The answer invariably is 'fear of getting hurt' or 'fear of disappointing others'.

When I further probe them, what comes up is so relatable and humane: fear of rejection, fear of losing control and not knowing what will happen, and the biggest of them all— fear of failure.

How do you handle fear?

Ignore it?

Find something to distract yourself like binging or partying?

Do not succumb to such numbing mechanisms. Do you want to challenge your fears? It will only harm you because you are delaying actions, which can shift the game for you.

Think about it.

Experiencing fear is normal. Even celebrities and world leaders have confessed to feeling anxious every time they had to deliver a performance or a speech. Feeling fearful is natural and human. You can definitely take small steps towards facing your fear and, in turn, build your muscle of courage.

Fear without action   *Fear with action*

Courage re-defined

It was a typical day at college for us BBA students. We were waiting for the bell to ring. Sharma Sir, our Economics teacher, asked the class a question pertaining to the subject. A few students tried to answer, but failed. I knew the answer but felt hesitant to put my hand up. Somehow Sharma Sir could sense this and asked me to answer the question. When I finally spoke, he said, 'That's exactly right. Why didn't you raise your hand and speak up earlier?'

I said, 'I thought I could be wrong because my answer was so different from everyone else and I was scared that my classmates might make fun of my answer.'

He heard me out, smiled and said, 'My dear, you need to have faith in yourself and, in the worst case scenario, even if you would have given the wrong answer, you would have learned from this experience.

'The beauty of life is that each experience is unique and teaches you something. Start with speaking in safe settings first, for example with your family and friends, and gradually open up in public settings to share your ideas. Mentally rehearse your ideas before going for an event or a meeting. You will begin to notice that repeated attempts of speaking will build your confidence and also enhance your appetite to take risks. _Taking risks is a critical part of building your muscle of courage_. Every time you take a step towards trying out something new, you build your muscle of courage to handle the unknown.'

I thanked him and made a note of the new meaning courage held for me now.

'Life shrinks or expands in proportion to one's courage.' (Anais Nin)

Courage = Showing up and having faith in your ability to handle the unknown and even if you are unable to handle it, you will be fine.

Ask yourself the following three questions that can help you handle any kind of fear:

What is the worst that can happen if I confront my fear?

What actions can I take to avoid the worst-case scenario?

What will be the financial and emotional implications if I don't take this action NOW?

Regret: What? When? Why?

In 1995, a leading psychologist Thomas Gilovich of Cornell University wrote the famous article 'The Experience of Regret: What, When, Why'. It was based on a study in which he asked people to look back on their life and list those things that they did but wish they had not and those things that they did not do but wish they had. The findings showed that most people regretted not becoming the person they wanted to be (their authentic self), or for not doing things they wish they did.

Bronnie Ware is a nurse who spent several years working in palliative care, caring for patients in the last few weeks of their lives. She recorded their dying epiphanies in a blog called *Inspiration and Chai*, which gathered so much attention that she put her observations into a bestselling book called *The Top Five Regrets of the Dying*.

Here are the top five regrets of the dying, as witnessed by Ware:

1. I wish I had the courage to live a life true to myself, not the life others expected of me.

2. I wish I hadn't worked so hard.

3. I wish I'd had the courage to express my feelings.

4. I wish I had stayed in touch with my friends.

5. I wish I had let myself be happier.[4*]

Do you plan to have any of these regrets? No? Then act now because actions happen in the present moment, *not* in the past or future.

---

4. Susie Steiner, 'Top Five Regrets of the Dying', *The Guardian*, 1 February 2012, https://www.theguardian.com/lifeandstyle/2012/feb/01/top-five-regrets-of-the-dying, accessed on 9 August 2022.

Both your past and future depend on your today

I love these lines Pema Chodron penned in her book *The Places That Scare You*: 'We can let the circumstances of our lives harden us so that we become increasingly resentful and afraid, or we can let them soften us and make us kinder and more open to what scares us. We always have this choice.'

Past is gone, future is not here, *hence present is the only moment you have*.

How to make the most of it?

You have to display courage in the present, let go of the past and build the muscle of not worrying for the future. Many people regret not making that phone call or standing up and speaking up when it mattered or taking up a new opportunity. *Do you too*?

'We spend so much time being afraid of failure, afraid of rejection. But regret is the thing we should fear most.' Trevor Noah could not have put it better.

Fear is unavoidable, but we can tame it by developing a friendly relationship with it.

Are you a success or a failure?

'You can't let your failures define you. You have to let your failures teach you.' Barack Obama

Do not attach your identity to the outcome of a particular situation. For example,

'If this project does not work, I will be a failure.'

'If they do not agree with my ideas, they will see me as a non-creative person.'

Do you think along these lines?

DON'T.

Your identity and the outcome of a situation are two different things. A project's failure does not make you a good or bad person. Learn from this experience and implement the learnings in your next project instead of regretting not even having tried. You are worthy and wholesome irrespective of the outcome of your project. Do not let failure or *success* define you.

The same funda applies to relationships. Do not accept 'no' from someone as rejection instead see it as redirection to something or someone better.

How do you view yourself? Do you think along the following lines:

- *I am an introvert.*

- *I am an extrovert.*

- *I am not courageous.*

Do you give yourself any of these labels?

DON'T!

Try to explore outside of these labels because they can be limiting. Do not say, 'I am fearful.' Say, 'I am experiencing fear, or I am feeling anxious.'

Dr Susan David, author of the bestselling book *Emotional Agility,* a leading psychologist at Harvard Medical School, puts it aptly, 'You are not your feelings. We own our emotions, but we are not our emotions. When we create space between how I feel in all my wisdom and what I choose to do in a values-aligned action, we generate the pathway to our best selves.'[5]

And whenever in life you feel that you are unable to handle a particular emotion or fear on your own, do not hesitate to seek support.

Most of my personal breakthroughs happened when I sought help and when I did not receive help from an expected source, I told myself that *they said No to my request, not to me as a person.* This motivated me to knock on one more door for help. These four words, *'I need your support'* can be life-changing. Try it.

5. Susan David, Twitter post, 10 August 2021, 9:02pm, https://twitter.com/ SusanDavid_PhD/status/1425117869227053063.

And keep reminding yourself time and again that the outcome of a situation does not define you. Your identity and outcome of a situation are *not* related.

Now imagine you were at a grocery store and the product that you were looking for is unavailable. What would you do? You will try to visit another store if you need that item badly, right? You will not take no for an answer from the first store personally.

Similarly, next time if someone is unable to help you, simply ask someone you trust for support and do not take their refusal personally. A study by Matthew D. Lieberman, professor and social cognitive neuroscience lab director at the UCLA Department of Psychology, Psychiatry and Biobehavioral Sciences, reveals that when you verbalise your emotions, like fear, sadness, anxiety, helplessness, you feel them less intensely. You could either write down your emotions, or talk to someone you trust. This will help you to feel better. If you can name your emotion, you can *tame* your emotion.

Remember, everything you are feeling or experiencing now, will be gone soon. Your feelings are not permanent because there is light at the end of every long, dark tunnel.

Imagine you were sitting in a room that suddenly plunged into darkness, now you could continue to sit in the dark, or you could switch on the lights. The same holds true with your fear. You need to face your fear to develop courage and it takes courage to face your fear. 'Because everything you want is on the other side of fear.' (Jack Canfield) Once you identify the feeling behind your fear (emotion), you can discover ways to handle it.

Naming the feeling	Support needed to face your feeling
Fear of being ridiculed to	Call your friend/colleague to hear you out/take their perspective

Bending the curve of fear

Professor Brian R. Little, a professor at Cambridge university is a pioneer in the study of personality, motivation and well-being and has redefined the way people look at their personalities. He suggests that one can transform oneself as one's personality is not fixed.

Do you think you are not courageous?

There is good news for you. Your personality is evolving, so you can fear less some day.

Ask yourself:

What scares me?

- *Is it speaking in front of my boss?*
- *Is it fear of losing a relationship?*

- *Is it losing my hard-earned money?*

- *Is it fear of rejection or being ridiculed?*

- *Is it fear of trying something new or flying or bungee jumping?*

If you said 'yes' to any one of these questions or for that matter all then let me extend my congratulations to you for being human. Take a leap of faith, choose courage not fear and take action. The ability to take action is in *your* hands. If you procrastinate, your fear will grow over time. Are you living your life on this curve where fear is increasing over time because of no action?

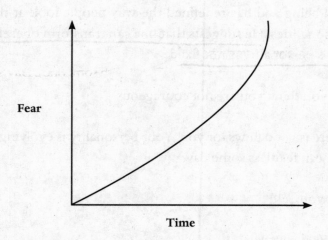

When you respond to fear at an early stage in its growth by taking an action, it recedes.

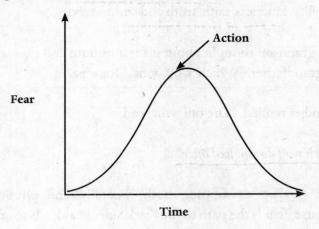

From messy to mesmerising

Never commit the mistake of comparing your journey with someone else's. Everyone is dealing with their struggles in their own way. Do not compare your Day 5 with someone's Day 500.

You can never know by just looking at someone's life story, what self-monitoring tools they are using, or how they got out of a messy situation. Acknowledge the challenge you are experiencing and ask for support. This way, you choose to make your life mesmerising instead of messy.

Let me share a story that I often narrate in my training sessions. Once an old man was explaining to his young grandson about the inner battles of humans. He said, 'My son, the battle is between two "wolves" inside all of us. One is evil and it represents—fear, anger, jealousy, sorrow, greed, false pride, superiority and ego. And the other wolf is good as it represents courage, peace, joy, humility, kindness, faith, truth and compassion.

The grandson thought about it for a minute and then asked his grandfather, 'Which wolf wins, Grandpa?

Grandpa replied, 'The one you feed.'

Which wolf do you feed often?

Fear can be devastating both mentally and physically. Because 'fear is the path to the Dark Side. Fear leads to anger, anger leads to hate, hate leads to suffering.' So said the wise Jedi master Yoda in *Star Wars*.

We fear things when there is uncertainty. Fear is often caused due to a lack of trust in ourselves.

Take a moment to list three things that you have been wanting to do in your life but postponing. What actions are required to do them?

....

....

....

....

....

What is stopping you?

....
....
....
....
....

What is your brain tricking you to believe?

....
....
....
....
....

There will never be a perfect or right time to start something, the only time is NOW because what has gone cannot be changed, and we can never possibly know what will happen in the future, what we can surely do is to take an action NOW. The more you explore what you are afraid of exactly, the less power it will have over you and you will build your courage muscle.

Shrink or SPREAD?

Your mistakes do not matter that much to others as much as you think it does. Researchers at the University of Cincinnati in a fascinating study concluded that 85 per cent of the things we worry about do not happen in real life and the remaining 15 per cent of things happen in a way that are manageable. Next time when you face a fear try to explore what is on the other side.

Silence is golden, really?

Both you and I grew up believing that silence is golden. It could be sometimes. But is it wise to stay silent when you have something important to say? Don't be afraid to share your ideas. 'The brave man is not he who does not feel afraid, but he who conquers that fear.' And Nelson Mandela should know what he is talking about!

The statement 'your work will speak for you' was valid more than a decade ago, but the world has changed. People will always have an opinion about what you say or do. So, do it anyway. A research by the late John L. Colley, a pioneering professor from the University of Virginia Darden School of Business on courage states that the reason we see courage in short supply is because we are biologically programmed to avoid risks and harm to ourselves. We prefer playing safe rather than standing up even though the long-term consequences of our action could be bad for us. He adds that we can build the muscle for courage by exploring the risk involved and taking actions in situations where risk is low.

I often do a role-play exercise with my clients called Courage Rehearsal. We create a situation wherein they are experiencing fear and we rehearse how their courageous self will act in that situation. At the end of the role-play, I always tell them that while it is critical to show courage, it is equally critical to understand when to let go—not every situation requires of you to show courage. I am reminded of these beautiful lines by C. Joybell C., 'Choose your battles wisely. After all, life isn't measured by how many times you stood up to fight. It's not winning battles that makes you happy, but it's how many times you turned away and chose to look to a better direction. Life is too short to spend it on warring. Fight only the most, most, most important ones, let the rest go.'

Just because certain things have not turned out the way you wanted, it does not mean they will not turn out better in the near future. A NO from life should be seen as *not yet*.

In testing moments, take a pause and ask yourself: *How would I show up if there were no consequences*? The answer can change the way you look at life, and more importantly, how you look at yourself every single day.

Once a journalist asked Mahendra Singh Dhoni, 'How do you keep yourself so cool?'

Dhoni replied, 'Simple, don't think about the result. It's the result that puts pressure on us. What if this happens, what if we don't win the game...what if we don't get selected...But we should worry about the controllable, take care of it. You may get the desired result and if you don't get the desired result you will improve, redesign your plans and execute better in your next opportunity. Thinking about the result never gives you result, you can have a target in mind but what is important is to take care of small steps in life and that will help you to thrive.'[6]

Do not be afraid to take risks in order to make things happen for yourself. Why?

Do you want to blame yourself for the rest of your life that you did not give it one more try?

Think of things you are afraid of and ask yourself why you are afraid of those things?

I am afraid of ....because ....
....
....
....
....
....

Now think of the actions that are within your control; I call them the inner ring. If you feel you are unable to find a way out, think of some people who can guide you to move

---

6. The Startup Show, 'M.S Dhoni explains how he stays cool during hard situations', YouTube, https://www.youtube.com/shorts/SojpUrYH61s, accessed on 23 September 2022.

forward, they are in your outer ring. These steps may appear small, but every such action takes you a step closer to your goal.

Inner ring ....

Outer ring.....................................

Whom do you admire?

We admire those who are not afraid to let their guards down, who are not afraid to be vulnerable, who are open to share their struggles and who are honest about who they are. In other words, people who are not afraid of being their authentic self. How do you know that you are not being your authentic self?

Well, your body gives you several signs. You know that tension that you feel inside when you say something to hide the truth? That is your inner guiding power (IGP) telling you that you are not being authentic. When you are doing things to please people or to seek their approval/validation, or when you do not express your honest opinion in front of them—you are not being your authentic self. Each aspect of your personality relates to some value of yours. Acknowledge and express that.

The most basic and simple example of authenticity can be seen in kids. A child does not fear showing up as they are. If they do not like the food they have been served, they will show their dislike by not eating it. No matter how they feel, they freely express it.

Have you noticed how a kid could be crying at one moment and start smiling a few moments later? A child knows that emotions are not permanent. *You were like that too.* And then you grew up. If you keep avoiding your authentic feelings, you will create a pile of pent-up feelings, only waiting to explode in the future. God knows on whom.

Now you may argue that children act authentically because they have not discovered the complexity of emotions yet. Are emotions really complex, or do we just believe them to be? What do you think?

Being yourself does not mean you never censor yourself or you never stop yourself from saying or doing certain things. I am not encouraging you to be rude or impulsive. Being yourself or being authentic means you are not pretending to be someone else to impress people.

When you operate from authenticity, you know that the core of your being is love and being authentic also means operating from love.

Have you ever done something that felt fantastic in that moment, only to regret it later? Seeking instant gratification is the worst form of self-harm. This happens primarily when you are not in a healthy relationship with yourself. An important part of building a healthy relationship with others is building a healthy relationship with yourself first, and that is possible if you show up fully as you are.

No one has or will ever have the exact combination of your talents, skills, thoughts, life experiences and this is exactly what makes you unique. When you make it absolutely okay to be yourself, then you also allow others to be okay to be themselves.

Authenticity has become the buzzword nowadays. You must have often heard the catch-phrase, 'I was just being myself' from a friend or may be you used it often too, but at times we use this phrase to defend our behaviour that is demeaning of others. Adam Grant puts it beautifully, 'I was just being myself' is an excuse for disrespectful behaviour. Authenticity without empathy is selfish. Be true to your values but show regard for others' values too.'

Some questions that you could ask to check why you are hesitating to show up as yourself are:

What threat am I perceiving that stops me from showing up as who I am?

What beliefs/thoughts are preventing me from accepting myself?

What feeling is getting triggered when I am trying to be my authentic self?

What is at stake?

When you are true to yourself, it allows you to connect with yourself in a more meaningful way. When something in your life does not feel comfortable, ask yourself: *What actions can I take to show up as myself without compromising the other person's dignity at the same time?*

The path to being your authentic or courageous self is being comfortable with making mistakes, taking a few missteps as they are part of the journey of progress.

There will be occasions when you look back at life and ask yourself: *Why was I not being authentic or courageous in that situation*? Please have a lot of compassion and love for yourself for making that choice. Maybe at that time your options or understanding of the situation were limited.

Courage is not about fearlessness all the time, it is about taking action even though you are scared. Also, fear is your friend. Yes, you read that right. Fear is a friend who gives you a signal to what you are resisting. I am reminded of a dialogue from the movie *The Good Dinosaur* where Poppa says, 'Sometimes you gotta get through your fear to see the beauty on the other side.'

Think about your life for a moment. As you look at times that you have taken risks, I am sure you have experienced fear in those moments, fear of the opinion of others or fear of change or fear of failing but you took the plunge any way. Many a time, what holds us back is not so much the opinion of others but our own thoughts. When you leave attachment from the outcome and focus on the process, you channelise your energy into what is possible in that moment rather than worrying about what is not.

Just being themselves is the biggest fear people have because they have lived their lives trying to satisfy other people's demands. Many have conditioned themselves that to be accepted they have to follow other people's point of view.

If you count yourself among them, then it is important to acknowledge this fear before you can conquer it. Fear is the root cause of why many people do not want to be themselves or are afraid to share their ideas with others. And the only way to conquer any kind of fear is by facing it.

Courage Slip

I ....(your name) give myself the

promise to act on..

....

....

....

....

....

A popular Chinese proverb says that the best time to plant a tree was twenty years ago. The second best time is now. Similarly, the best time to have tackled a hard problem was a long time ago; the second best time is now.

Muster the courage to move forward. Marianne Williamson beautifully describes the innate power we all have in her bestselling book *A Return to Love*: 'Our deepest fear is not that we are inadequate. Our deepest fear is that we are powerful beyond measure. It is our light, not our darkness that most frightens us.

We ask ourselves, "Who am I to be brilliant, gorgeous, talented, fabulous?" Actually, who are you not to be? You are a child of God. Your playing small does not serve the world. There is nothing enlightened about shrinking so that other people won't feel insecure around you. We are all meant to shine.'

Fear-less Zone

Take a moment to jot down three of your biggest fears and steps you commit to take to face them.

....

....

....

....

....

....

....

....

....

COMMIT TO YOURSELF: REAP OPTIMUM BENEFITS

As you come to the end of this book, I want to convey my heartfelt thanks to you for trusting me in this process. Here are some concluding thoughts to ignite a spark in you.

Remember: Life happens. And *shit* happens. There will be distractions and temptations, but do not forget the reason you embarked on this journey of tapping into your highest potential in the first place. I am sure that one day, you will share your story of unlocking your potential with others and become a source of inspiration for them.

We often receive notifications on our laptop and phones to update apps and softwares for better functioning. When was the last time you updated yourself? Or, are you still living in the old programme?

Let me emphasise here again, before you work on your relationships with others, you need to work on the relationship you share with yourself. In this process of self-discovery, do not feel guilty for keeping yourself before others. Change may appear uncomfortable at first, but no change has ever happened for people being in their comfort zone. If you feel stuck at any point in your life, start by taking a small step or action for your highest good. 'What the caterpillar calls the end of the world, we call a butterfly. (Eckhart Tolle)

I am reminded of a beautiful line from the bestselling book *Way of the Peaceful Warrior* in which 'Socrates' puts it aptly, 'The secret of change is to focus all of your energy not on fighting the old, but on building the new.'

Your number one responsibility is to take care of yourself first. When you are alone, you are with yourself. When you are with someone, *you are still with yourself*. You are the person who wakes up with yourself. When you take care of your needs first, you are making yourself a priority and building a capacity to take better care of others.

We all know that we are going to die one day, but nobody takes it seriously else we would show up differently every single day of our lives. Sometimes later becomes never and NOW is the best time to begin and to commit to an everlasting journey of growth—moment by moment.

All success comes from internal peace (I) and has little to do with external situations and people. What you want to become is entirely up to *you*. No one is going to come to save you because you are capable of saving yourself.

If not now, then when?

It is time to start living the life you imagined for yourself, NOW.

Love and light.

SELECTED BIBLIOGRAPHY

Books

Berne, Eric. *Games People Play:* Penguin, 1964.

Branden, Nathaniel. *The Six Pillars of Self-esteem: The Definitive Work on Self-esteem by the Leading Pioneer in the Field.* Bantam, 1995.

Chodron, Pema. *The Places That Scare You: A Guide to Fearlessness in Difficult Times.* Shambhala, 2002.

Clason, George S. *The Richest Man in Babylon.* Fingerprint Publishing, 2022.

Clear, James. *Atomic Habits: An Easy & Proven Way to Build Good Habits & Break Bad Ones,* Avery Publishing House, 2018.

Coelho, Paulo. *The Alchemist: A Fable about Following Your Dream,* HarperCollins, 2018.

David, Dr Susan. *Emotional Agility: Get Unstuck, Embrace Change, and Thrive in Work and Life.* Penguin UK, 2017.

Dobelli, Rolf. *The Art of Thinking Clearly.* Hachette UK, 2013.

Kiyosaki, T. Robert. *Rich Dad, Poor Dad.* Time Warner, 1997.

Krishnamurti, J. *Freedom from the Known.* Rider & Co., 2010.

Mackesy, Charlie. *The Boy, The Mole, The Fox and The Horse.* Ebury Press, 2020.

Millman, Dan. *Way of the Peaceful Warrior: A Book That Changes Lives.* HJ Kramer/New World Library, 2009.

Murphy, Dr Joseph. *Believe in Yourself.* Manjul Publishing, 2015.

Miralles, Francesc and Garcia Hector. *The Book of Ichigo Ichie: The Art of Making the Most of Every Moment, the Japanese Way.* Quercus, 2020.

Ruiz, Miguel Don. *The Four Agreements: A Practical Guide to Personal Freedom.* Hay House, 2017.

Tolle, Eckhart. *The Power of Now: A Guide to Spiritual Enlightenment.* New World Library, 2004.

———. *A New Earth: Awakening to Your Life's Purpose.* Penguin UK, 2009.

Tolstoy, Leo. *A Confession.* Merchant Books, 2009.

Ware, Bronnie. *The Top Five Regrets of the Dying: A Life Transformed by the Dearly Departed.* Hayhouse, 2017.

Williamson, Marianne. *A Return to Love: Reflections on the Principles of "A Course in Miracles".* HarperOne, 1996.

Winfrey, Oprah. *What I Know For Sure.* Pan Macmillan, 2004.

Yogananda, Paramhansa. *Autobiography of a Yogi.* Om Books International, 2017.

Websites

Google. 'Privacy Policy.' Privacy & Terms. Last modified 17 April 2017. https://www.google.com/policies/privacy/

Yale University. 'About Yale: Yale Facts.' https://www.yale.edu/about-yale/yale-facts, Last accessed 1 May 2017.

Ackerman, Courtney E. 'What is Attachment Theory? Bowlby's 4 Stages Explained.' Published 27 April 2018. https://positivepsychology.com/attachment-theory/. Last accessed on 3 October 2022.

Amabile, Teresa M. and Steve J. Kramer. 'The Progress Principle: Using Small Wins to Ignite Joy, Engagement, and Creativity at Work.' https://www.hbs.edu/faculty/Pages/item.aspx?num=40692. Last accessed on 3 October 2022.

Begley, Sharon. 'The Brain: How The Brain Rewires Itself.' Published 19 January 2007. http://content.time.com/time/magazine/article/0,9171,1580438,00.html. Last accessed on 24 December 2021.

Cosan, Zeynep. 'Paradox of Choice.' Published 21 September 2020. https://www.leidenpsychologyblog.nl/articles/paradox-of-choice. Last accessed on 21 December 2021.

Detert, James R. 'The Practice of Courage.' Published 22 June 2021. https://ideas.darden.virginia.edu/practice-of-courage. Last accessed on 20 January 2022.

Feinblatt, Natalie. 'If It's Hysterical, It's Historical.' *Inclusive Therapists* (blog). Posted on 20 February 2020. https://

www.inclusivetherapists.com/blog/if-it-s-hysterical-it-s-historical#:~:text=The%20saying%2C%20%E2%80%9CIf%20it's%20hysterical,a%20favorite%20food%20of%20yours.&text=You're%20no%20longer%20able%20to%20get%20your%20favorite%20food. Accessed on 12 March 2020.

Keep Your Brain Alive. 'Neurobics, The Unique New Science of Brain Exercises.' http://www.keepyourbrainalive.com/. Last accessed on 3 October 2022.

Little, Brian. 'Who Are You, Really? The Puzzle of Personality.' https://www.ted.com/talks/brian_little_who_are_you_really_the_puzzle_of_personality. Last accessed on 3 October 2022.

MacLellan, Lila. 'A New Study on the Psychology of Persistent Regrets Can Teach You How to I've now.' Published 10 June 2018. https://qz.com/work/1298110/a-new-study-on-the-psychology-of-persistent-regrets-can-teach-you-how-to-live-now/. Last accessed on 20 January 2022.

Michal (Michelle) Mann, Clemens M. H. Hosman, Herman P. Schaalma and Nanne K. de Vries. 'Self-esteem in a Broad-spectrum Approach for Mental Health Promotion.' Published 1 August 2004. https://academic.oup.com/her/article/19/4/357/560320. Last accessed 3 October 2022.

Nash, Jennifer. 'What are Your Personal Values?' Published 26 November 2020. https://hbr.org/2020/11/what-are-your-personal-values. Last accessed on 12 December 2021.

Nath, Sayantani. 'On 26/11, This 24-Yr-Old Woman Single-handedly Saved More Than 60 Lives.' Published on 17

September 2019. https://www.thebetterindia.com/195443/26-11-mumbai-attacks-taj-hotel-unsung-hero-woman-saved-sixty-lives-india/. Last accessed on 20 January 2022.

Perlow, Leslie A. and Jessica L. Porter. 'Making Time Off Predictable—and Required.' Published October 2009. https://hbr.org/2009/10/making-time-off-predictable-and-required. Last accessed on 3 October 2022.

Pine, Karen J. 'Self-acceptance Could be the Key to a Happier Life, Yet It's the Hobby Habit Many People Practise the Least.' Published 7 March 2014. http://blogs.herts.ac.uk/2014/03/self-acceptance-could-be-key-to-happier.html?m=1. Last accessed on 2 February 2022.

Waldinger, Robert. 'What Makes a Good Life? Lessons from the Longest Study on Happiness.' https://www.ted.com/talks/robert_waldinger_what_makes_a_good_life_lessons_from_the_longest_study_on_happiness?language=en. Last accessed on 3 October 2022.

Wolpert, Stuart. 'Putting Feelings Into Words Produces Therapeutic Effects in the Brain: UCLA Neuroimaging Study Supports Ancient Buddhist Teachings.' Published 21 June 2007.

https://boevinkgroup.com/2014/02/24/yes-85-of-what-we-worry-about-never-happens/#:~:text=Researchers%20at%20the%20University%20of,to%20turn%20the%20situation%20around. Last accessed on 21 January 2022.

Wikipedia. 'Attachment Theory.' Last edited 5 September 2022. https://en.wikipedia.org/wiki/Attachment_theory. Last accessed on 31 December 2021.

————. 'List of Cognitive Biases.' Last modified 30 September 2022. https://en.wikipedia.org/wiki/List_of_cognitive_biases. Last accessed on 17 December 2021.

————. 'Spotlight Effect.' Last modified 18 August 2022. https://en.wikipedia.org/wiki/Spotlight_effect. Last accessed on 3 October 2022.

Steinhorst, Curt. 'Rethinking the Value of Core Values.' https://www.forbes.com/sites/curtsteinhorst/2019/10/17/rethinking-the-value-of-core-values/. Last accessed on 3 October 2022.

Blog called *Inspiration and Chai*.

ACKNOWLEDGEMENTS

Every worthwhile task of my life has been accomplished with the valuable help of many individuals—and writing this book is no exception. I thank my husband Vikas and daughter Ishita for being my pillars of strength and sounding boards.

Mom and Dad, Ila, Nikhil for being my backbone and asking a million times in my journey of writing this, 'When is your book getting published?' It helped me maintain my focus. Thank you Father-in-law and Mother-in-law for all your love and support.

A biiiiig thanks to the Chief Editor of Om Books International, Shantanu Ray Chaudhuri, for being kind, patient and encouraging throughout the journey. I have learned a lot from him in all our interactions. Special thanks to Jyotsna Mehta for being warm, understanding and supportive throughout the editing process. It was the best team to work with.

To my powerful inner circle of friends and well-wishers— you know who you are—thanks for teaching me the things that I needed to learn, saying the things I may not have wanted to hear but needed to and believing in me on the days I did not believe in myself.

Finally, a big thanks to myself for taking the journey that helped me discover that life really does work best when it is lived from the inside out . . .